Dark Clouds Don't Stay Forever

Memoirs of a Jewish German Boy
in the 1930s and 1940s

Werner Neuburger

PublishAmerica
Baltimore

ISBN: 1-4137-9776-8
PUBLISHED BY PUBLISHAMERICA, LLLP
www.publishamerica.com
Baltimore

Printed in the United States of America

This book is dedicated to the three women who banished my clouds and let my sun shine: my mother, my sister and my wife.

Contents

Foreword

Several years ago, when my youngest son, Daniel, and his wife, Ann, had their first child, Erica, they gave me a book entitled *Grandfather Remembers — Memories for My Grandchild*. The book consists of inquiring statements that required completion by filling in the blanks. As such it had to be quite general in nature. Although it covered all sorts of topics, I felt I needed to tell my story with more emphasis and specifics: my experiences in Germany during the insidious growth of the Hitler era, why and how I came to America, and how I evolved to become an American. I felt the need to tell the story not only to Erica, but to all my grandchildren and to their families, and for that matter, to the world. And so I started to write my memoir. I was aided by photographs, letters and documents that have survived. Our oldest son, David, and his wife, Marilyn, visited my birthplace, Battenberg, where they obtained a copy of the roster of families residing in that village in 1929. That also helped to refresh my memories. I've tried to tell my story as best I can recollect and believe it to be fairly accurate.

Aside from my personal story, I've attempted to convey an understanding of how the evils of Nazism took hold in Germany, a civilized society; how these evils affected millions of innocent people, destroying their livelihood and the very lives of many. Yet those who escaped from that hell, as I did, and were fortunate enough to end up in the United States, had the opportunity to forge a wonderful new life. If I've conveyed that, then I have succeeded.

—Werner Neuburger

Prelude

It was during the long winter evenings in Vineland that, at my prodding, my mother told me extensively of my father's early life; how she and he met, and of their early life together. Sometimes, when she was thus reminiscing, my uncle Sigmund, the catalyst of their long ago meeting, leaned forward from his easy chair and good naturally added a few facts and thoughts.

My father, Louis Neubürger, was born and grew up in the village named *Battenberg an der Eder* (on the Eder River), in the German state of Hessen-Nassau. Battenberg consisted of about two hundred houses and a population of slightly over one thousand souls. Most of the boys of Battenberg were his friends. He was just like all of them, with one exception. He was Jewish, and in addition to attending public school he went to Hebrew school every Sunday morning in Battenfeld, a neighboring village. That was however inconsequential. He didn't go to church on Sundays, but then neither did many of his non-Jewish friends. The religious orientation of Battenberg was predominantly Evangelist, with a few Catholics and five Jewish families.

As he grew up in Battenberg, he was sought out for his ability to fix almost any malfunctioning mechanical item, primarily bicycles. He owned tools and had a basic comprehension of the complex new freewheeling mechanism with which the bikes were equipped. He repaired the bikes free of charge, which made him sufficiently popular to be invited to join the elite bicycle club as one of the youngest members. The bicycle club was gloriously named EDERGOLD of BATTENBERG. With uniforms consisting of blue suits, yellow caps, matching sashes, and with an ornate flag staff holding the club's rigid banner, they had won numerous awards, and never failed to participate in any of the local parades. Quite a sight with their wheels and handlebars bedecked with greens and flowers.

When the great World War started in 1914, he was twenty-three years old. He and his friends, without hesitation, volunteered for enlistment en mass and were trained as a unit, proud members of the 24th Jäger Battalion of the Third Corps. They were the Battenbergers from the *Eder Tahl* (Eder River Valley), and they were proud of it. They were renowned for their camaraderie, their esprit de corps and lack of fear—or maybe it was blind patriotism. They were *Hessians*, tough soldiers. Soon after their training in Marburg, they found themselves at the Western Front, facing the French troops. Inevitably many were wounded, including Louis, whose eardrum was damaged by a nearby exploding shell, which also filled his left arm full of shrapnel. Unable to move that arm and bleeding profusely he was evacuated to a field hospital in Königswinter. There he spent almost half a year and regained substantially full use of his now slightly shortened arm. The hearing loss would never be restored. Since he had a fully functioning right ear, the partial hearing loss was not a very serious handicap.

After his recovery, Louis was assigned to a military selection team whose job was to assign new recruits to specific army units. When he received a brief furlough, he returned to Battenberg. He expressed his interest in wooing Helene, a nineteen-year-old woman he had met through his brother-in-law Sigmund. However, his mother, Rosetta, would hear

Louis Neubürger, 24th Jager Battalion, 1914.

nothing of it. Helene was much too young. "Wait until she's grown up, then if your infatuation endures and after due process, then—we'll see." Louis felt strongly but not strongly enough to overcome his mother's iron will. He did however maintain a correspondence that suggested that when the war was won, they'd celebrate together.

The war was not to be won, although there seemed to be no end to announcements of victories. In August of 1918, a major German army offensive at Marne failed. In September, omens of doom became realities when Bulgaria, one of Germany's allies, signed an independent armistice. Soon, the Ottoman Empire (Turkey), one of Germany's stronger allies, did likewise. In early November, the Austria-Hungarian Empire signed an armistice. The handwriting was on the wall. A Germany starved and defeated without allies, and short of munitions was too much for Kaiser Wilhelm the 2nd. Although his proverb throughout the war was *Lerne zu leiden ohne zu klagen!* (Learn to suffer without complaining!), he heeded the respected General Hindenburg's advice. He abdicated his throne and fled to neutral Holland. On November 11, 1918, Germany signed the armistice. The war was over!

Louis and the millions of other disheartened warriors returned to their respective homes as best they could. With food and money in short supply, and with few jobs available, life was almost unbearable through the winter of 1918–1919. Living in a farming community, however, at least there were potatoes for the stomach and wood for the oven. After a very bleak winter, spring arrived with the promise for a new start.

Louis attempted to stay in touch with Helene by mail, but even the once highly efficient mail service had broken down. Letters seemed to take forever to get to their destination. In the summer of 1919, Louis hoped to visit Helen in her hometown of Framersheim and cement his friendship with her. Framersheim, in the district of Rheinhessen, was occupied by the Allies, as was most of the Rheinland area of Germany. Travel was extremely

Helene Schloss (my mother), circa 1918.

difficult, especially for ex-German soldiers. They were required to have travel authorization from all the Allies they would encounter along the way. A visit from Battenberg to Framersheim required authorization from both the Americans headquartered at Coblenz and the French at Mainz. It was not until fall of 1919 that Louis succeeded in getting the necessary passes and amass enough funds to proceed with the trip. At the first checkpoint he was stopped and sent back. His French authorization, which he had gotten first since it was more difficult to obtain, had expired. Discouraged and frustrated, he returned home. Repeating the effort, he finally succeeded in 1920, arriving in Framersheim in time to help with the grape harvest.

Helene's father, Heinrich Schloss, had a small clothing store, but his main income was derived from a substantial business importing cork for wine bottles. He also had several vineyards, a grape press, and a wine cellar. During the brief period of grape harvesting, every able-bodied person was recruited to help. Women and children cut the grape bunches with scissors and placed them into pails. The men had large buckets strapped to their backs and walked up and down the rows of grapevines to have the pails dumped into their buckets. They then carried the grapes to large wooden vats mounted onto horse-drawn carts. At the end of the day that harvest was brought to the courtyard at home for processing.

Louis very much enjoyed helping with the harvesting and was pleased to be heaped with compliments, not only by Helene's parents, Heinrich and Rosa, but also by her brother, Walter. After two weeks, Louis returned home, looking at the world with new vigor and confidence. Helene was everything he had hoped for, and she was now twenty-one years old.

The proceeds from the family store in Battenberg were barely enough to support the family consisting of Louis' mother and two unmarried sisters, Lene and Else. His father, Isidor, had died several years ago. His younger brother, Salli, was still a dependent, attending dental school. However, his two older sisters, Nanni and Herta, were married. After much thought and consultation with his two brothers-in-law, Sigmund and Julius, who each owned a successful store in Korbach, a town not far away from Battenberg, Louis decided to visit farmers in nearby villages where there were no stores. He enticed these new customers with the offer to deliver their orders. At first, he did this by bicycle and later with horse and carriage. Using the store as a home base, he slowly expanded the enterprise, making it relatively profitable.

The farmers he visited seemed to appreciate the service. They were busy six days a week working the land and had little time to go shopping. On Sundays all stores were closed. Louis expanded his product line to meet their needs and the needs of the Battenberger customers. He could now supply not just cloth for clothing, bedding and curtains, but *Colonialwaren* (wares from the "ex" colonies) such as coffee, tea, sugar, spices. Furthermore, a special skill he had developed, permitted him to offer the service of repairing centrifuges. These were pieces of equipment almost every farmer had to enable him to separate cream from milk, thereby improving the yield of cream from which butter was churned. His natural skills also allowed him to repair whatever else needed repair. He also sold tools and hardware. Throughout this time he did not ignore his local friends; he joined the hunting club, the volunteer fire brigade, and continued his membership in a bicycle club. Best of all, he kept up an active correspondence with *"liebe, gute Helene."* To her he confided his concerns, frustrations and aspirations and assured her that as soon as possible they would share their lives together.

In 1922 they met again in Korbach. This seemed to be the appropriate meeting place with a sympathetic chaperone and a good place to announce their engagement. The world looked very positive now, except for the growing inflation. Every week the Deutschmark became less valuable. What might have cost 1 mark this week cost 2 marks the next week and 4 marks the week after. Within a few months all savings had lost their value. If

1,000 marks had been saved, it would only buy a loaf of bread. A few weeks later a loaf of bread would cost 100,000 marks. And yet life must go on. Louis and Helene finally married in November 1923, after the grape harvest and before winter.

For their honeymoon, they made a trip to the North Sea resort island of Nordernai. This was the first trip to the ocean for either of them. Perhaps not the best choice at this time of year since it was cool and windy, but the rates were very attractive since it was past high season. Anyhow, there was something romantic about the rhythm of the ocean that neither had experienced before. After several days of leisure at the Nordernai Beach, they returned home to Battenberg to start their new life together.

By then Lene, Louis' younger sister, who still lived at home, recognized that Battenberg would not be her future home. An event the year before had established an idea in Lene's mind. The previous summer, "Uncle" Sigmund Langsdorf, a cousin of Isidor, had visited the Battenberg homestead.[1] Uncle Langsdorf was a successful merchant in New York, in the United States. He was intrigued with the attractive and spirited young lady, Lene, and encouraged her to think about coming to America. He had just the man for her to marry and would take her under his wing. In 1924, the man whom Uncle Langsdorf had earmarked for her came to visit in Battenberg. He was Nathan Simon, an impressive stately gentleman. He had a very pleasant disposition and immediately made a hit with Lene and the whole family. Before long, Lene's emigration to America became a reality. There the wedding was sponsored by none other than Uncle Langsdorf.

It was heartbreaking for Mother Rosetta to consider that her beloved Lene would be as good as gone forever. Little did she or anyone realize that in years to come, Lene would save the whole

------

[1] Sigmund Langsdorf was the son of Samuel and Johanna Langsdorf. Sam was the brother of Nannchen, Isidor's mother. She (Nannchen) and Levi Jehuda Neuburger were Isidor's parents, my (Werner's) great grandparents.

Neubürger family from the ravishes of the Holocaust. Little did anyone know that Battenberg, which had been the ancestral home of the family for hundreds of years, would not remain the family homestead much longer.

Edergold Bicycle Club of Battenberg
My father is third from right (hatless).

Chapter 1

Helene and Louis, Inge and I

Within the confines of the house in Battenberg, a new pattern of living evolved. Helene tried to blend her lifestyle with that of her mother-in law, Rosetta, but became quite frustrated. Rosetta wanted things to be done the way they had been done in the past. Every activity was scrutinized and criticized. Rosetta might say, "We always washed ourselves with cold water," while Helene used warm water for her morning wash. "Warm water is just a waste of fuel." Cooking, baking, mending, ironing laundry, bleaching the linens, beating the carpets clean, raking the courtyard, washing windows, starching the curtains—every domestic endeavor brought forth differences in the way these matters were to be handled.

Louis spent most of each day traveling to neighboring farm communities where there were no retail stores. Each evening when he came home he tried to console a distraught Helene and assure her that in due time things would evolve her way. They talked of the future and their aspirations. Louis dreamed of enlarging the house to give each of the women more private space. Enlarging the store would allow him to hire a sales

Our house in Battenberg just prior to the new addition.
Mother (Helene),Oma and father (Louis) in doorway.
Note bricks for new construction at side of house.

trainee (*lehrjunge*) and establish Helene's control of the store. Since Rosetta was selling the merchandise she had kept when Louis took over the store, she in effect operated a competing business. Louis knew that eventually Rosetta would run out of merchandise, and she was not inclined to restock, especially in the light of the extensive inflation. Time was a crucial factor. With loving kindness, Louis persevered, and little by little, Helene saw the light at the end of the tunnel. Their mutual affection and compassion culminated in the proud moment when Helene, after a visit to the local doctor, Gustav Winkler, also an army buddy, announced that she was pregnant.

In 1924, inflation was getting worse by the week and there was no escape. Farmers and workers were at a complete loss to handle the ever more challenging finances. Business people could only keep track of transactions by converting any monetary value into equivalent American dollars. Compared to the almost worthless German mark the dollar was rock stable. A loaf of bread might cost a million marks this week but worst of all next week it would cost twice as much. Thousand and million mark certificates were practically worthless. Into this unreal world, Helene gave birth to their first child on August 31, 1924. Her name was Ingeborg, a good German name that reflected Louis and Helene's optimism for Germany's future and their declaration to be part of it. Ingeborg's birth eased the tensions at home and convinced Louis to expand the house as soon as the financial situation would permit.

That winter was a difficult one financially since inflation had reached a point where a loaf of bread cost many billions of marks. Most people had a very hard time doing the high level arithmetic necessary for the minimum of buying, selling or even counting their wages. The government continued to be deadlocked, and the German people were still suffering from the consequences of the wartime defeat. Friedrich Ebert, the elected German president was finally defeated in election and replaced by Field Marshal Paul von Hindenburg.

1927. Left to right; my mother, Sigmund Stahl, Nathan
Simon, Nanny Stahl. Ludwig Lowenstern, Lene Simon,
Herta and Julius Lowenstern, Louis (my father).

Our house after renovation, 1928.
Left to right: Paul (apprentice), Mariechen (maid), Louis,
Oma Rosa (my grandmother), Inge, a neighbor,

Hindenburg, the military hero of the war, was highly respected by most Germans. He succeeded in rallying the nation and was able to obtain from the war victors the help necessary to start a new currency system, which ended the long period of inflation. Things started to look up. Of course, everyone's bank savings had been wiped out.

A new government, a new optimism and a new spirit of equality emerged. Louis joined with other forward-looking Battenbergers to create a new life. He was still a member of the bicycle club *Edergold*. He also was a member, as were most of his army buddies, of the hunters club (*Schussverein*), the war veterans (*Kriegsverein*) and the volunteer fire brigade. As much as possible, he gave fellow Battenbergers credit for essential purchases if they could not pay in cash. He had faith in the integrity of his neighbors. He was not disappointed since they attended to their obligations as promptly as they could. There was little charity in Battenberg, but there were also very few deadbeats. Everyone took their obligations seriously.

Ingeborg, now called Inge, had her first birthday. She was an adorable child and received the munificent love and attention that further nourished her. With things looking positive, Helene and Louis decided to have another child and hoped that it might be a boy. When Helene told Louis that she was pregnant again, Louis decided to realize his dream of expanding the house. In front of the existing house, which had two stories and an attic, he added a three-story addition with modern plumbing and central heating. I was born September 7, 1926 while this new construction was still underway.

This is where my story begins!

Chapter 2

My Early Recollections

Down the full distance of my memory, my earliest recollections are of my being awakened, from what must have been an afternoon nap, by the noise of stone chipping. When I climbed to the edge of my crib, or perhaps it was a junior bed, I watched with fascination the re-cobbling work being done on the street outside our house. A group of stone workers picked up each new rough six-or-so-inch cube-shaped stone and chipped off the edges so that the stone would fit perfectly against another to form a slightly arched curve from curb to curb. Apparently, the old stones had become so smooth over the years of use that the horses, pulling loaded wagons, especially after it rained, would slip and fall on their knees. I did not then know the reason for the re-cobbling, but the stone workers' procedure must have made an indelible impression on me since even now I can still visualize the team of workers, each with a burlap screen angled to retain the chips. Each man wore safety glasses and sat on a one-legged stool, chopping away at the stones. They did this for hours on end without interruption.

Inge and I at the base of the Burgberg.

My crib and later my bed was in the room next to my parents' bedroom. I shared this room with my sister, who had her bed along the wall adjoining my parents' bedroom.

It was said that I was not as dynamic as my sister. My father, in an attempt to get a reaction out of me, would crumble a newspaper and tear it apart, hoping I would copy him. Apparently, I was content to just rest and not bother doing anything that required an effort. I did not start speaking as early as my sister, nor did I use the potty. It was much easier not to bother.

My second recollection is of my first friend, Lotti Schneider, who was almost my age and lived next door. Her father was a shoemaker. He also had two older daughters and a younger son. One daughter, Emi, was as old as my sister. They were also best of friends. Liesel, who was substantially older, often took the role of baby-sitter, telling us what to do and what we could not do. She captivated our little group by reading to us from our book of Grimm's Fairy Tales. We sat in a row on our sofa, entranced by her dramatic presentation. Lotti, Emi and Liesel spent much time in our house, and we in theirs. When we were not indoors, we usually played in our yard or in our garden. Once, while playing in our yard—perhaps I was five years old, probably in 1932—a motorcyclist raced past our house and Liesel shouted at him: "Nazi, Nazi." I did not know what it meant, but I recognized the tone as being derogatory, and I joined in her outcry.

In those days, "Nazi" didn't mean anything to me. To some people in Battenberg it was a name given to "no-gooders" who disturbed the tranquility of the village by their occasional racing through the streets on motorcycles at speeds that were considered unsafe and uncivil. Occasionally I heard adults talk about those *ferdamte Nazis* (damned Nazis), who had no respect for the peace and quiet of the neighborhood. In those days, incidents involving Nazis were relatively rare in Battenberg, and were certainly insignificant in my daily life. In springtime

27

my sister and I joined many of the village children and adults for the annual festive exodus of the villages sheep, lead by a community shepherd. We accompanied him and his sheepdogs to the edge of the village. There were many hundreds of sheep, practically all of Battenberg's sheep, which were individually marked to identify the owners. The shepherd, with his wagon-like shelter on wheels, took the sheep to distant meadows where they would graze the entire summer under his solitary guidance. Occasionally in the summer our parents would pack a picnic lunch and we would hike to one of the sheep meadows to keep the shepherd company for a little while. Petting the woolly sheep and chasing them was fun. The shepherd, all by himself most of the time, would always welcome company and we enjoyed his playing of the harmonica as he encouraged us to accompany him by singing. At home, my sister and I had a continuity of pleasant occasions. I remember helping my mother plant potatoes. They had to be cut up so that each piece, which was to be planted in the soil, had a sprout. We learned how to harvest asparagus by watching Mother. When radial cracks appeared in the surface of the smooth sand mounds in which these plants were cultivated, we knew the white asparagus shoot was about to break through the surface. Once through, the exposed part would turn green, and so it was harvested while still tender and white. Mother made every garden task an adventure.

I also remember our neighbor, the banker's wife, Frau Stark, a pleasant, full bodied, well groomed woman, who frequently came to our store to purchase items and occasionally bought a candy (*Zuckerstein*) and gave it to me. An extremely warmhearted person, she was always very friendly. She once told my mother, in my presence, that she loved this little boy and wished she could adopt him for a little while. I was thrilled with the idea of playing in their big house across the street. My mother wanted to test me and said it was up to me. I said "yes." Mother suggested that I pack my pajamas and toothbrush, which I did cheerfully. I said goodbye to Mother and walked with Mrs. Stark across the street and up a slight hill to their home, the bank building. The bank offices were on the first floor and the living quarters on the second floor with bedrooms on the third floor. Mrs. Stark was older than my mother and had a son who was grown up and away. I believe he attended a university. She took me to his room and pointed out that this could be my room, and I could play with the toys therein. I did and had a great time exploring all these new items. After a while, Mrs. Stark called me and said, "It's time for afternoon cake and milk." What a utopia! After that, she suggested in her warm sing-song voice that we go down to the bank and say hello to Mr. Stark. I did not know him since he never did any shopping in our store. I rethought my "adoption" and decided I'd rather go home. "Well," she said, a bit more firmly, "in that case, I better give you something to take along." She gave me a big piece of cake and a few candies "for the road!" I remembered to say thank you, whereupon she complimented me on my good manners and wonderful behavior and told me that I'd be welcome to visit again anytime.

Many families in Battenberg were similarly friendly. I recall a Mrs. Hermine Beil, a ruddy-complexioned, hefty, but warm-hearted person. She was called Reh Hermine because it was said that she once caught a deer (*Reh*) in her back yard and without regard to her personal safety, helped the excited animal get back into the woods. She used to visit us and bring butter-laced cookies for Inge and me. Spengler Schmitt was a short, but muscular sheet metal fabricator whose shop was just a few houses away from ours. When we visited there, he encouraged us to play with some of the scraps of metal and showed us how to use a hammer and pliers. He showed us how to shape metal on an anvil and finished our efforts by converting our scrap into a basket or privet or an ornament.

Prune jam season was almost a festival in Battenberg, and an apt occasion for playing pranks on the children. I remember once it was suggested I go to neighbors to borrow a small glass ladder, supposedly to permit us to climb into the large (about three-foot diameter) wash kettle turned prune kettle after most of the prune jam was removed so that we could lick the remainder of this delicious fresh jam. I diligently ran to the neighbor, who advised me that they had just lent their glass ladder to the family across the street. I followed the trail across the street only to discover that they had further lent the elusive ladder to the *Bürgermeister* (the mayor) who lived just around the corner from us. I continued the search for the elusive ladder. When I confronted the mayor's wife, she thought that she had returned it to our house, and thus, I began to realize that the search was in vain. There was no glass ladder. However, in the course of my search I did receive several cookies as reward for my perseverance. So it all was not really in vain. Life generally seemed to be an ongoing series of pleasant events. The sun seemed to shine forever; no dark clouds yet.

Father's business had become more profitable, and he hired an apprentice, Paul Hess, an athletic, curly-haired recent high school graduate, to help in the store. For training as a merchant, he received room and board and a small stipend. To help my mother, we hired a maid, Mariechen Kotchalk, the daughter of the village wood chopper. Mr. Kotchalk was a tall sinewy fellow who split logs into firewood stakes. He chopped wood for a living day after day, steadying the tree section on the chopping block with his left hand while swinging the ax with his right hand. Each fall he chopped a years supply of wood needed for our kitchen stove. He chopped enough wood to fill a wood shed in our back yard. Often, as I watched him, hypnotized by his smooth repetitive motions, I would stare at his left hand which had half a thumb missing, "The result of a mis-chop a long time ago," he told me. He did not speak much, but often repeated that line. Mariechen lived with us. She helped clean the house, do the laundry, and she learned to cook under my mother's guidance. In her free time she played with us.

Shortly before I turned six, my father met with the head teacher of the Battenberg school regarding my prospective enrollment. The school had three classrooms and three teachers. One teacher taught the first four years of school, one the fifth and sixth grades, and one the seventh and eighth grades. The latter was the head teacher (*Hauptlehrer*). He thus doubled as teacher and principal. He knew my father well and suggested that since I would be one of the youngest students in class, it might be a good idea to wait until I was closer to seven years old before starting first grade. There was no kindergarten. In view of the turbulent politics going on in Berlin and other cities in Germany, and the problems arising from large unemployment in Battenberg as well as everywhere else, it seemed prudent to give me the benefit of a little more maturity. The hope was that in another year the political turmoil would settle down. Although I didn't personally feel any of this turmoil, there were serious problems at that time in Germany. Dark clouds were drifting in.

———◆◆◆◆———

After World War I, the German government was reestablished as a republic. A constitution was drafted in the city of Weimar, hence, the new republic was known as the Weimar Republic. The constitution declared equal rights for all citizens and universal suffrage. On paper it was an ideal constitution that contained an extensive bill of rights, including freedom of speech, and proportional representation. This new freedom, rather than uniting the German people, unleashed passions on all sides. Assassinations were not at all uncommon. Right wing anti-republicans took advantage of the freedom afforded by the constitution to form a paramilitary organization, the "Free Corps." They took it upon themselves to dispense justice "gun in hand." They and their sympathizers justified their actions as a response to the recently signed Versailles Treaty, which they considered unacceptably humiliating. They called the German negotiators criminals. They were upset that part of the state of Prussia was ceded to Poland, that two entire states, Alsace and Lorraine, were ceded to France, and that Germany's overseas colonies were distributed among the victors of the World War. In addition, Germany's army was limited to 100,000 men but could have no airplanes or tanks and was forbidden to enter the Rheinland, the part of Germany west of the Rhine river. The Treaty also required "exorbitant" reparations (132 billion marks) to be paid. Left wingers were primarily Communists, who saw Russia as their role model. They succeeded in obtaining control of some localities, and for a short time they obtained control of the state of Bavaria. That of course incensed the right wingers much more. The right wing parties obtained the support, especially the financial support, of industry, which was mortally afraid of the Communists.

To help the small middle-of-the-road parties to counter the extremists on both sides, politically active Jewish centrists formed the *Central Verein* (Centrist's club). My father, although not politically active, was in sympathy with their concept of "Primary Jewish loyalty to Germany" and joined passively as did most of his Jewish friends and relatives. Most Jews were liberal and more in sympathy with the Socialists and Communists than with the right wingers, who were also more vocally anti-Semitic.

The pacifist attitude of a great many Germans did not hinder the Free Corps. In 1922, Germany's Jewish foreign minister, Walter Rathenau, was assassinated. He was murdered by men of the extreme right who hated him for being a Jew and for attempting to carry out some of the national obligation of the Versailles Treaty. These rightists acknowledged Hitler as their spiritual leader. An astute and outspoken Jewish Communist leader, Rosa Luxemburg, was brutally assassinated with her non-Jewish colleague, Karl Liebknecht. They had been successful in organizing a soviet-type Council of People's Representatives, but Free Corps troops crushed the Council, arrested its leaders and killed them. Shortly thereafter Bavaria's Jewish Socialist premier, Kurt Eisner, was murdered by a young right-wing officer.

By the early 1930s the country was more politically divided than ever. President Hindenburg, by now in his 80s, could no longer cope with the rising economic and political difficulties. As the result of the world depression, unemployment had increased dramatically. In Germany, a country of about 65 million people, where the work force was about 16 million men, the unemployment was about 6 million, over 37% of the labor force. As in the rest of Germany, in Battenberg there were opposing political groups and many unemployed. Universal bickering and suffering affected Jews and non-Jews, but it seemed to be slightly more focused on Jews.

By this time, a group that refused to accept Jews as genuine fellow citizens and calling itself the "German Workers Party" sought out like-minded Free Corps militants and other extremists, and changed its name to the "Nationalist Socialist German Workers Party" (NSDAP), commonly known as Nazis. Their leader was Adolf Hitler. Hitler was born in Austria into an unhappy family. He had a tyrant of a father and a mother who was 22 years younger than his father. Adolf experienced very little happy family life. He was a failure at secondary school. He broke his relationship with his father and went, full of rancor, to the Academy of Art in Munich. There he achieved nothing and so went back to Vienna where he was rebuffed on all sides. He grew to hate the environment that did not understand and did not accept him. In Vienna, he ended up in an asylum and subsequently did just about anything to earn some money. During this desperate time, he came in contact with strong reactionaries and learned to despise almost everyone and everything, including Jews, capitalism, communism, democracy, foreigners and the government as he knew it.

He volunteered for the German Army because he believed that Austria was too decadent, too weak, and too liberal. In his view, only the "Aryan" Germanic nation was fit enough to succeed. "Conscience," he said, "was a Jewish invention." The only thing that counted for Hitler was the indomitable will, hard as steel. Only the strong had the right to lead and command and the strong were the Aryan Germans.

Hitler's group had attempted to take over the city of Munich in 1923 and had failed. He was arrested and jailed. While in jail he wrote *Mein Kampf* (*My Struggle*). In it he defined his principles: anti-capitalist, anti-Bolshevik, anti-criminal and most emphatically anti-Semitic. He stated his plans to unify all European Germanic peoples into a Greater Germany at the expense of whoever got in the way. He claimed that Germany had the right to expand (*Lebensraum*) because they were a superior race. The Jews were to be removed because they were an alien race which was international in outlook and interest, and therefore not supportive of his goals. Hitler saw the world as a jungle in which the strongest ruled, and the strongest were the pure Aryans (the master race). In this jungle, the Germans would get, by any means necessary, that to which they were entitled.

Battenberg had a very small contingent of NSDAP members. When Battenberg was relatively prosperous—from about 1925 to 1930—they were laughed at. But in the early '30s, when farmers could not make a living and when unemployment increased, many indebted farmers and jobless men went to their meetings and saw in the NSDAP cause a cure for their personal misfortune. The NSDAP was promising relief from farm debts and work for all, to be obtained at the expense of the internal enemies of Germany. Their Robinhood-like promises to take from the bad rich and give to the good poor appealed to the poor, who thought themselves good.

Meanwhile, the Weimar Republic had deteriorated. In March 1930, when President Hindenburg asked the middle-of-the-road Chancellor Bruning to form a new cabinet, extremists from both the Nazi right and Communist left rioted in the streets and were subdued with great difficulty. In September 1930, the NSDAP, also known as the Nazi Party, was able to collect six million votes and thus received 107 out of about 500 seats in the *Reichstag* (the German Parliament).

Von Hindenburg was reelected president in 1932. Within a short time he suffered the resignation of three chancellors. On January 30, 1933, he was induced to make a fatal decision, thanks to the intrigue of politicians, the impotence of political parties, and the urgings of the military elite and Communist-fearing industrialists. Hindenburg appointed Hitler chancellor (prime minister) of Germany.

As soon as Hitler was in control, he used his party's protective teams, the S.A. (*Sturm Abteilung,* or Storm Detachment) to create havoc among his political enemies. In February 1933, the Reichstag building burned to the ground. Based on the claim that the Communists did this as their signal to stage a revolution, he asked for and received "temporary" special dictatorial power, which allowed him to suspend constitutional civil liberties, freedom of speech, the right to assemble, freedom from search as well as suspension of privacy of postal and telephone communications. Thus empowered, a wave of arrests followed.

In March 1933 a new election was held, and although Hitler received only 44 percent of the vote, none of the several opponents came close to obtaining that large a percentage. With Hitler's new "mandate" the Reichstag was dissolved and he could now implement his plans with the help of the S.A. and the newly formed S.S. (*Schutzstaffel* or Protective Echelon).

Trade unions were banned under the rationale that they were Communist infested. Strikes were forbidden since all workers were now enrolled in the National Socialist Labor Front. Workers were guaranteed job security but could not change jobs without government permission. Farmers could not be removed from their land because of debt, but they also were not allowed to leave their farms for other jobs. Political parties were banned. Jewish civil servants were dismissed. All this occurred with little resistance, thanks to the efficiency of the S.A. and S.S. and the German concept of obedience. On the first of April 1933, all Jewish stores were to be identified by posting S.A. men at each store entrance. The S.A. men urged potential customers to boycott Jewish establishments.

This type of boycott occurred at increasingly frequent intervals.

———•••••———

It was on that sort of day in the fall of 1933, on which the school year started, and I was to go to school for the first time. Wearing a brand new sailor suit and with my new schoolbag on my back, my father asked me to pose in front of our house so that he could take a picture of my first day at school. I was very excited and most willing to pose. As we stepped outside our house, an S.A. man stood post in front of our store. The S.A. man, who's name I do not recall, was a familiar Battenberg native. He was perhaps thirty years old and was in full uniform, brown shirt and brown jodhpurs with knee-high boots. A diagonal shoulder strap was secured to his heavy belt which also held a holstered pistol. The stiff-sided cap equipped with a chin strap made him look taller than he really was. His attire included the standard red arm band with the black swastika in a white circle and swastika emblems on his cap and shirt collar. His very presence at our store entrance intimidated most potential customers from entering the store, but when a potential customer edged his way towards the store, the S.A. man would rattle off as if by rote: "Don't buy from Jews. If you are a true German, you will not buy from Jews." At this time, anti-Semitism in Battenberg was more abstract than personal.

Despite his dour message to passersby, he politely moved aside for the photo session, either because that situation was not covered by his instructions or out of respect for my father, whom he knew well and against whom he had no personal animosity. He hesitantly apologized, stating that he was a good German who had no choice but to obey orders. Inwardly my father was infuriated, but he reasoned that this was an action ordered by the government and this government, like the others before it would not endure for long. He felt that the noble Hindenburg would not tolerate this injustice on top of all the other recent injustices. When it was time for me to actually walk to the school that morning, my mother and father had a mild debate whether I should go to school in view of the action occurring in front of our house. Mother preferred to have me stay home to avoid any possible incident in school. After all the enthusiasm I displayed to start school, she did not want me to start with a negative experience. My father, however, still had faith in the community. This after all was Battenberg, where he had always been respected. Also, he felt that giving in to our fears would cause me to miss the first day of school and thus start a chain reaction that might cause me more trouble in the end. He knew Frau Ruppel, my teacher, quite well and felt confident that she would be fair and proper. My mother shared the confidence in Frau Ruppel, and so both soon agreed that the appropriate thing was for me to go. Since there appeared to be few customers coming to the store, my father would accompany me.

I was anxious to go, having been envious of my sister who had already gone to school for two years. I did, however, have a lot of apprehensions, not only those that might be typical of a first day of school student, but also because I witnessed debate by my parents as to the wisdom of sending me to school under "these" circumstances, which I really did not understand.

School was about a ten-minute walk from home. I was relieved to see as we walked that some of my friends who also were going to school for the first time were likewise accompanied by a parent or older sibling. We reached the large school grounds in the center of which stood the brick school building, one of the largest structures in Battenberg. We climbed the steps to the central lobby, and in a moment we were in one of the three large classrooms. This was the combination classroom that also served as the first grade. Frau Matilde Ruppel, my new teacher, warmly greeted everyone including me. I had often seen her in our store, and she gave me what I felt was a special hug and she assured my father that in her classroom there would be none of this Hitler stuff. She was an experienced teacher, a hefty woman, probably in her early forties. Her hair was neatly coiffured into a bun at the back of her head. Her smiling round face with large eyes exuded a warm disposition which immediately made me feel at ease.

The bell rang. The parents were asked to leave, and school started. One of the first questions Frau Ruppel asked was when we each had our birthdays. She seemed to know everyone by first name, or so it seemed to me. I knew my birthday well, but the poor fellow sitting next to me could only identify his birthday by the fact that it occurred during the potato harvest season *"im Doffelausmachen."* The other students subsequently berated him, giving him the nickname "Doffelausmacher." I felt sorry for him, and we became friends, perhaps not only because I felt sorry for him, but because I felt that my other classmates were not as friendly towards me as I expected. Doffelausmacher came from an extremely poor farm family that lived in semi isolation on the outskirts of the village, and thus he had little social contact with the other children of Battenberg. There was only one Jewish student other than myself in the class, Hannelore Stern. She was tall and pretty with her long black braided hair but was quite shy. Since our parents were distantly related and were friends, we quickly felt comfortable with each other. We soon became best of friends.

During the first weeks of our school year, Frau Ruppel captivated our interest by reading each day an installment of the story *The Life of Phali the Phalbauer*. Phali was the name of a mythical early Teuton who lived in a home built on stilts at the edge of a lake with a drawbridge to protect him. He was the perfect example of an ideal German: strong, brave, blond, hardworking, and self sufficient, yet obedient. After school I sometimes lay on my back in the cool grass between the trees in our backyard meadow, looked up at the sky and studied the ever-changing cloud formations, imagining myself a buddy of Phali. What I did not realize was that most of the neighborhood children I used to play with seemed to be unavailable when I wanted to play with them. Even Lotti, my best friend in the neighborhood, seemed to be less available then she used to be. Hannelore and sometimes Doffelausmacher, in their own way, were more reliable playmates.

Since Battenberg was a small community of about one thousand inhabitants, there was only one first grade, and all students who started together would stay together as a class as they advanced through the grades. Frau Ruppel would be our teacher for four years, and we would remain in the same classroom for that period of time. At grade five we would transfer to another classroom and another teacher. For now the security of Frau Ruppel's warm demeanor assured me of a pleasant school experience even though a large picture of Adolph Hitler hung above the chalkboard at the front of the classroom.

The boycott of the store by the S.A. men did not vex me as much as it afflicted my parents, but I recall one event in 1934 that imparted a deep impression on me. It was a mass book burning. One evening in spring there was a spectacular torch-light parade. The marchers included the recently formed Battenberger Young Folk, the pre-teenaged boys organization, the Hitler Youth (HJ), boys were aged thirteen to eighteen, as were the B.D.M.—*Bund Deutscher Mädel*, the girls league. The marchers also included a large number of S.A. men (brown shirts). They all were dressed in their respective uniforms and sang more or less in unison as they marched to the center of town, which happened to be within easy view of our house. In their formations they must have had over one hundred torches. These consisted of poles wrapped at the top with straw and rags, tied to the poles with baling wire, and soaked with kerosene prior to being lit. Many of the marchers who did not carry torches or flags carried piles of books and papers. As the marchers reached the open area next to the small triangular park in the village center, the intersection of Hauptstrasse and Marburger Strasse, located in front of our house, they ceremoniously piled up the torches to form a bonfire and then sequentially threw the books and papers into the fire. My parents, Inge and I watched from behind our second floor living room windows. Cheers and songs accompanied the book burners' activity. I could not imagine how there could be that many books in all of Battenberg, and I sensed my parents' disgust with this activity. I was stimulated by the torch lights and fire much like a child is stimulated by fireworks. Yet I was confused and puzzled since books were such a valuable commodity in our life, and I did not understand why this was happening. How could they burn such respectable and valuable items as books? I saw that my father was visibly shaken. He kept repeating the word *unglaublich* (unbelievable). Hearing him repeatedly express that thought only added to my bewilderment. Mother tried to explain to us that Hitler was causing something to be done that was very wrong, but we could not do anything about it. This was a new and strange and incomprehensible concept for me. At that time I did not realize that this was just one of the acts by which German culture was being subjugated to the propaganda policies of the Nazis under the pretext of Germany's rejection of the "subversive and degenerate intellectual culture." I did, however, realize that books, an item held in high esteem in out family, were being destroyed. Over and over the thought ran through my mind,"How could they burn such respected items as books?" In fact, writings by such people as Thomas Mann, Albert Einstein, Jack London, Upton Sinclair, Helen Keller, H.G.Wells and hundreds of others whose writing was considered subversive and alien to German thought were condemned to the flames in this and similar bonfires throughout Germany.

I recall one of the first times the Jung Folk (younger boys organization) marched past our house. I was standing in our yard and as I watched them. I held back tears for I envied their uniforms, their spirited singing and their apparent camaraderie. Why could I not be part of that? I knew I was Jewish, but why did that bar me? It was one of the first times I had the feeling of inferiority, of being an odd ball. One of my first dark clouds!

One day in August 1934, in my second school year, Frau Ruppel came into the classroom very sad. She told us of the terrible news that the great President Hindenburg had died. "This would be a day the world will never forget," she told us. Several days later she brought into the class a postage envelope with a stamp showing the face of Hindenburg with a black overprinted border. She advised us that when we got home, we should collect and save such stamps. This would be a once-in-a-lifetime occasion to get stamps that eventually would be rare and valuable collectors items.

When I came home, I told my parents of this unique opportunity. My father located several stamps with different denominations all with the countenance of Hindenburg and black overprinted borders. My mother gave me a few straight pins, and I carefully pinned the stamps to a piece of paper. This was the beginning of my first stamp collection.

A few months later, when cousins Hans and Ludwig Löwenstern visited us with their parents, it was Ludwig, three years older than I, who enlightened me. "Stamps only have value if they are completely intact. Even a pinhole makes them worthless." I discarded my worthless collection and started another one.

Whenever our relatives from Korbach, the Löwensterns and the Stahls, visited us, the whole family would go for a substantial walk to the Burgberg, the wooded hill behind Battenberg. Atop this hill there remained the ruins of a castle once inhabited by the Battenberg (Mountbatten) family. The path we usually took spiraled through a shady forest, around the mountain, terminating at the top, at the ruins. We usually took a steeper but more direct trail back down to the village. On our way up, we children loved to run ahead and play hide and seek in the remains of the moat and the ruins of the castle, consisting primarily of a tower. Nearby, a small refreshment stand was the meeting point where the children and adults would reunite. We were usually on our best behavior because we knew the reward for being good was a chocolate-covered marshmallow-like cookie for each of us.

Frau Ruppel must be credited with noting that I had problems with my eyesight. She advised my parents to take me to an eye doctor in Marburg, which they did. The trip to Marburg, just my father and I, thrilled me beyond reason. There had been few occasions where I had my father all to myself for any length of time. To boot, this was my first train ride. After we got off the train in Marburg, I proudly kept pace with his steps, which seemed to me to be at a somewhat hurried pace. And when we entered the doctor's office, there were items of equipment that startled me. I thought that I had entered the world of the future. I was somewhat embarrassed when the diagnoses turned out to be: crossed eyesight, because my right eye was weak. The prescribed remedy was to cover my good left eye with a patch to strengthen my weak right eye. I found the patch to be rather restricting and shifted it for visual comfort so I could peek under it. Unbeknownst to me however, my cheating caused my right eye to further weaken so that when I got older my right eye lost most of its function.

Occasionally my father would set up his tripod and photo camera and take pictures. I envied his skill at this apparently magic art. Cameras were not common in Battenberg. His camera used specially coated glass plates instead of film for negatives. He developed the glass negatives in an improvised dark room in the attic. Once the glass plate negative was fixed, he used wooden frame holders equipped with spring clips to hold the print paper and negative in close contact and exposed this assembly to direct sunlight. The length of time exposed was related to the brightness of the sun. I remember him standing by the open window with the photo package in one hand and his pocket watch in the other. Since he took the pictures, he seldom appeared in them. He did however try to teach my mother to master this art of photography. Considering the crudeness of the process, it is surprising how well his pictures came out.

At that time, to me, Battenberg did not seem to be a bad place to grow up. Even if most of the neighborhood boys of my age played with me much less frequently than they did in the past, I had an ample coterie of friends. There was Lotte, the girl next door, whom I now sought out somewhat more than she sought me. Hannelore, my classmate, with her two neatly braided long black pigtails and an upbeat disposition had become my constant companion. She was always available to join me in any little adventure. We would climb the cherry tree in our backyard orchard, to eat our fill of Bing cherries just before they were harvested. Together, we'd take my small wooden wagon into the woods to collect pine cones, which both our families used as kindling for the kitchen stoves. Or we might enjoy the special thrill of joining our mothers to go to the meadow along the edge of the woods, or even in the leaf strewn woods itself, to collect wild mushrooms. Hannelore and I soon became adapt at identifying eatable versus poisonous mushrooms, but no mushroom could go into the "take home net" until our parents inspected them to make sure they were safe to eat. Our mushrooms included white champignons with the delicate pink gills, and yellow chanterelles which we called *Pfifferlinge*. Then there were the gray morels that grew among the leaves. Their cups looked like cone-shaped sponges, pitted like honeycomb. Eating meals prepared with these morsels always added an extra pleasure since we were recognized and lauded for having contributed to the meal.

In regard to other playmates, Gisela was a slightly younger second cousin who was always anxious to play with us since she had few other friends. Other playmates included my sister Inge and her friend Emi. Sometimes, and as a last resort, there was Doffelausmacher. I also had Flock, our dog. Robert Fingerhut, an older boy who lived across the street, would occasionally condescend to let me play with him and his friends. Robert's mother was a World War I widow who made her living as a seamstress. Since my father and Mr. Fingerhut had been in the army together, my father had special compassion for her and often gave her deep discounts when she purchased food staples in our store. My father often showed generosity to ex-army buddies who were unemployed or underemployed or not sufficiently successful at farming to make ends meet. Although my mother was generally in sympathy with him, she sometimes questioned his largess in view of our own needs. Nonetheless, his feeling for the Heimat was strong as was his love for Battenberg and of his country.

The store apprentice, Paul Hess, received a small salary but also got room and board as well as the use of a bicycle. Paul often gave me rides with me sitting on the handlebars. Once on such an occasion, a chicken walking on the street panicked and fluttered into our front wheel. I catapulted off the bike and onto the street. Aside from a few scrapes, I hurt my nose rather badly. It turned out I had broken it, and as a consequence I still have a nose slightly crooked to the side. This incident did not diminish my enthusiasm for experiencing the thrill of the wind in my face, as I moved rapidly as is wonderfully possible on a bike. I was not quite tall enough to reach the pedals, but with Paul's encouragement and guidance, I learned to ride the bicycle by positioning my body with a slight twist on the left side of the bike and pedaling with my right leg under the crossbar that connected the seat to the steering column.

Undoubtedly, this unsafe mode of biking influenced my parents to buy me a small bicycle for my eighth birthday. My sister Inge managed to cajole me into sharing the bike, which we used with great pride and joy. I don't believe that there was another children's-sized two wheeler in all of Battenberg.

My eighth birthday was also special because Uncle Salli had come to visit us in a stylish Studebaker convertible automobile, a huge American-made vehicle that drew the attention of the entire neighborhood and then some. He gave Inge the book *Pooh Der Bär* (*Winnie the Pooh*) and gave me the book *Petra Poesierlich* (*Charming Petra* [the Bear]). We had very few books of our own, so this was quite memorable. When Uncle Salli tried to explain that Inge's book was actually an English tale and mine a Swiss one, I was certain that he was wrong. When I offered a wager to support my contention, he accepted. My proof was that the books were written in German so the stories must be German. He suggested that I ask no less an authority than my schoolteacher to be the judge. Much to my dismay, but to my further education I lost the wager.

Chapter 3

The Hitler Impact Begins

April 20 was Hitler's birthday. In past years the day had gone unnoticed in Battenberg, but in 1934 it was different. Since Hindenburg's death, Hitler had assumed the title of *Führer* and Reich chancellor and had abolished the presidency. He was now a full-fledged dictator, and woe to the German who would not pledge and live in full allegiance to Nazi chauvinism. A popular slogan then was: "Adolph Hitler is Germany."

On the occasion of Hitler's forty-fifth birthday, flags were to be flown in his honor from every building. Flags that were prefabricated were not very common, and those that were available were relatively expensive. The more conventional means of acquiring flags, especially in small communities such as Battenberg, was to have them sewn by local tailors. To make a swastika flag, which the Nazi party had selected as the new national standard, required red material for the main field. A white circle of cloth was then sewn into the center of the red field and black cloth was used to create the swastika in the center of the white circle. This was a more involved task than producing the former German flag, which consisted of rectangular strips of black, red and gold cloth. Battenbergers had no intention to be lacking in the demonstration of support for the government, and at least two dozen flags were needed for Battenberg's public buildings and major street intersections. It fell upon *Rappelgeorge*, the official town crier, to purchase the material and commission the local resident tailors to sew the material into flags.

Since Battenberg had no local newspaper, and many farmers could hardly read, it had been the custom to have local announcements made by a town crier. Rappelgeorge, whose real name was George Jakobi, was a war veteran with a badly deformed arm. His official title was *Gemeindendiener* (community service man). Every day he received a list of community notices, ordinances, meeting notes of organizations, and any other items of local and national interest. He had a large brass bell that he carried with great decorum under his arm. Leather leggings added authority to his otherwise slight demeanor. At every street intersection in Battenberg—there were about eight of these—he would stop, ring his bell and with an authoritative stance that resembled Mussolini's, he would read announcements with a loud and clear voice. We, the children, loved to follow him and listen even though most announcements had no meaning for us. It was fun to watch him make his declarations to whatever bystander came near to listen. Almost as though it were a title of honor, everyone who did not call him George called him Rappelgeorge. Since he was the community service man, the task of flag material purchase was assigned to him.

George came into my father's store, enthusiastically advising my father that a sizable purchase was about to be made, and from whom other than his *Kamerad*. They had served together in the army. "After all, Battenberg should not be wanting when it comes to showing the colors."

My father refused. "George, how can you ask me to sell you material for those Nazi flags? Hitler is not even a German, and look how his S.A. boys are treating us! No, sir, you are not getting Nazi flag material from me!"

George was flabbergasted. "Louie, how can you do this to us? We really have hardly any other source for this material. We can't be without flags on Hitler's birthday! You are wrong in the way you are looking at the situation. Everyone in Battenberg respects you, and I assure you I will be the first one to stop anyone who gives you trouble. Those S.A. guys, they are just a confused bunch. They'd be the same whether there's a Hitler or not, but this is more than Hitler—it's about Germany. At last we have our own dignity again, people are working again, and the Communists are out of our hair. Times will only get better, and, Louie, we've got to have this flag material!"

My father stood firm. "No way, George. You underestimate how despicable the Nazi party is, and I will not be part of any of this. As soon as the Nazis are out of power, and I assure you that will be sooner than you think, I will be glad to donate the cloth for twenty black, red and gold flags. And that's final." Rappelgeorge's face turned red as a beet. He knew my father well enough to realize that my father meant what he said, and so Rappelgeorge stormed out of the store. Nonetheless, on April 20, Battenberg had its flags.

My father was quite proud of this action. He repeated this story often. Rappelgeorge soon thereafter joined the Nazi party and became one of its most rabid, rabble-rousing members.

I also recall the Battenberger drum and fife band, which had recently been formed under the auspices of the *Hitler Jugend* (Hitler Youth). The Hitler Jugend was somewhat similar to the Boy Scouts in the United States. They both championed outdoor life, their members were young boys with uniforms, and they were taught to live by their oath. However, the Hitler Jugend had a very severe political bend since its oath was absolute allegiance to Hitler, "the savior." Only Aryans were allowed to join, and they were required to do so. The oath was not idle but was administered with dead seriousness and was absolutely required to be observed to the letter. If a Hitler Youth overheard a slanderous remark by anyone, including any member of his family, he was expected without fail to report it to his leader. There was enough discipline in the organization to implement this sacred oath.

The uniforms were very smart with diagonal shoulder straps and a broad belt that held a sheathed knife. The recently formed Hitler Jugend of Battenberg had been advised to take advantage of available musical skills and improve their marching consistency by forming a drum and fife band. Its members were entitled to have a striped *appliqué* attached to the top of their uniform's sleeves. This was the same way German military band members were distinguished. The question of where to obtain the appliqués arose. Since our neighbor, Robert Fingerhut, was one of the band members and since his mother was a seamstress who could sew the appliqués onto the uniforms, Robert came to our store to inquire about the availability of the appliqués. This was not an item normally stocked in the store, but my father had catalogs of sources. My father supplied Robert with a catalog, so that a choice might be made whether these were to be black with white stripes or red with white stripes and whether they were to have fringes or not. Robert brought the catalog to the next Hitler Jugend (HJ) meeting, but when he identified the potential source, the troop leader informed him that these could not be purchased from a Jewish store. Reluctantly, a chagrined Robert returned to our store, embarrassed, as he told my father the instructions he received, and he apologized. My father nonchalantly let the matter drop until that evening when he expressed his concern that this Hitler situation may after all not be a passing fad. "The kids are getting infected by the Nazi propaganda." That was a bad omen.

Within a few weeks, my father was politely advised that it might be better for all concerned if he resigned from the bicycle club. Soon thereafter the hunters club and the volunteer fire brigade made the same request. Customers, and even friends, who formerly came through the store's front entrance started to come after sundown via the entrance at the side of the house. They said that they opposed what was going on but did not want to create any controversy. It seemed that no one dared to resist openly, and as isolated individuals, they felt powerless. The common expression was: "What can one person possibly do?"

Fridays were baking days in our house. Usually, every Friday, several large flat trays were filled with raw crumb cake dough and topped with sugary crumbs. We, the children, brought these to the nearby baker, Karl Traute, and after the cakes were baked in the large bakery oven, we picked them up. The cakes were always baked to perfection. The delectable wafting aroma of the freshly baked cake often tempted us into swiping a few of the delicious crumbs off the top on our way home. Once, however, the cakes were completely charred when we went to pick them up. Enraged, my mother returned to the bakery where she quickly got the message. The baker's helper who did the actual baking was a member of the Nazi party. Upon confrontation, *Bäckermeister* Traute suggested that henceforth, we would be well advised to bake only what would fit into our own wood stove. Here then was another example of a "good German" succumbing to the pressure of the Nazi anti-Semitism.

What made "good Germans" like Bäckermeister Traute succumb to his helper? What made Battenbergers, and for that matter typical Germans conform to the totalitarian Nazi policies and accommodate hostility towards the Jewish People? What made the Nazis "successful" in 1933 and 1934? At the time of these occurrences, I was puzzled. I did not understand why these events were happening.

Unlike the United States, Great Britain, and France, Germany did not have established democratic traditions. Germany, prior to 1871, was a loose confederation of a several sovereign states, principalities and cities states. Prussia, by far the largest, had it's own king and a strong, well-disciplined army and set the example for the other German states. Prussia lead the way at that time of Germany's fragmentation, to maintain rigid absolutism, complete and unrestricted power of the govern-ment. Prussia's rigid absolute rulers functioned not so much for the welfare of the subjects, but to enhance the state and to perpetuate its power and glory. Thus there was cultivated the proverbial German characteristics of diligent work, sacrifice, and subservience to authority. The German absolutism proved remarkably impervious to emancipatory currents. While revolutions swept away privileges based on birth in the United States and France, the Prussian Code of 1794 reaffirmed such privilege. In 1848, a major attempt at liberal constitutional government and limited monarchical sovereignty failed when Prussia's King Friedrich William IV used the army to crush the movement. Thus lost was one of the rare opportunities for Germans to set their country on the path to democracy. While economic changes were instituted, autocratic institutions remained firmly entrenched. In 1871, the German states were united and the Prussian king was crowned as the Kaiser over all of Germany. That throne claimed its power by divine right. German policy was declared to be "iron and blood" rather than compromise and majority rule. The absence of democracy was interpreted as a mark of superiority. German citizens were given a fertile environment for industry and economic development. In return, their duty in life was one of work, obedience, and sacrifice. The German government was benevolent but autocratic until the end of World War I.

When World War I ended in November 1918, Germany lost its Kaiser and its government. In this chaos, the Bolsheviks and their sympathizers attempted to establish a soviet-type government.

The Socialists, who were more conservative, and included many working-class leaders, usurped the existing political vacuum and arbitrarily proclaimed a republic in an effort to stop the leftists. The remnants of the royalty, military leaders, and the *Junkers* (the aristocratic landowners of huge estates in Prussia) considered this republic to be the lesser of the two evils. They had abdicated their own power when they were not willing to sign the armistice and the Treaty of Versailles. For the moment, they were willing to help the Socialists put down the anarchy and Bolshevism that had sprung up throughout Germany.

Following the proclamation of the republic, elections were held throughout Germany for members of an assembly that was to draw up a new constitution. After months of debate, the Constitutional Assembly, meeting in the city of Weimar, drafted a very democratic and liberal constitution. However, it included a system of proportional representation which made a stable majority in the Reichstag impossible. Numerous political parties evolved, and none could establish a majority. The result was frequent changes of government where stalemates occurred in the Reichstag over almost every problem that arose. The extreme left parties and the extreme right parties outnumbered the center parties, and majority coalitions could not be established. In the streets, the constitutional freedoms permitted inflammatory oratory that led to violence and local revolts. The fruits of this political stalemate were rampant inflation, excessive unemployment, and severe discontent throughout Germany.

Average Germans became disgruntled with democracy and longed for the good old days when the Kaiser ruled with benevolent authoritarianism that provided for relative prosperity and law and order. When Hitler proposed return to discipline, work, and a new establishment of order, he found ever increasing acceptance. I recall, as a child, that the word *democracy* was considered derogatory, much as the word *communism* was in the United States or as the word *capitalism* was in the Soviet Union. The slogan *Ein Volk, ein Reich, ein Führer* (one people, one nation, one leader) was a common expression of national aspiration that became heard ever more frequently in Germany from 1934 on.

Prior to 1933, in speeches aimed primarily at industrialists, Hitler insisted that he was the enemy of planned economy. He asserted that free enterprise and competition was absolutely necessary. Words like these attracted substantial funds and support, but once in control, he acted conversely and did exactly the opposite of what he said. In 1933 when his private army had more S.A.(storm troopers) and S.S. troops than the German army, he secretly plotted a forced takeover, but publicly preached change by constitutional means. Thus the then existing government did nothing to stop him.

One of his biggest lies occurred immediately after he was in power. He claimed to have proof that the Bolsheviks were about to overthrow the government and that they had set fire to the Reichstag as a starting signal. He finagled the Reichstag to give him legislative power to permit him to implement "defensive measures against acts of violence endangering the state." The Reichstag fire had been set by his henchmen, and the new supposedly temporary powers were immediately used to silence all the opposition and those who raised questions. Thousands were arrested, and opposition newspapers were suspended. Germans were able to read only news that reflected favorably on Hitler. He claimed to have saved the nation and the people, and receiving little evidence to the contrary, Germans believed him. Although he became a true dictator, the people were pleased to see restoration of discipline.

Another lie was Hitler's constant proclamation that he wanted only peace, not war. For example here is an excerpt from one of his speeches: "…Whoever lights the torch of war in Europe can wish for nothing but chaos…."[2] While proclaiming

---

[2] Hitler speech November 1934.

peace, he was actively rearming Germany. He increased the size of the armed forces from the legal limit of 100,000 to 500,000 and then to several million men. He created an air force in violation of the Versailles Treaty and embarked on a warship construction program of the greatest magnitude. Most Germans had their fill of war and were happy to hear him express peaceful intentions, but were not upset that he was building a strong Germany. They felt that a strong military added to the reestablished national self esteem.

Hitler claimed that the Jews were a materialistic international race that did not have the national interest of Germany at heart in the way that the superior Teutonic Germans did. This was generally accepted by the Germans since there was no proof presented to the contrary. The church had always said something similar by stating that the Jews were immoral because they did not accept the superior teaching of Christ and had killed Christ. The national press, now controlled by the Nazi party, strongly supported these claims and added the Nazi bias for good measure. Many Germans did not associate these claims with the individual ordinary Jews they were personally acquainted with, but did tend to believe that "big Jews" were in positions of power and were probably guilty of not supporting Germany. Germans had always felt that they were superior and Hitler's racial policy was not worth taking issue with. Anyway, the Jews constituted less than one percent of the German population, and opponents of the anti-Semitic policies were branded as enemies of the state. No sense looking for trouble! Those who were not enthusiastic about his anti-Semitic lies were not sufficiently organized to do anything effective and thus joined the chorus of those who said: "What can one person possibly do?"

At the end of the first World War, the German army was still positioned outside the borders of Germany and Hitler's claim that the army did not lose the war was palatable to many Germans. Whereas the Weimar republic government was handicapped by having ratified the Versailles Treaty, Hitler was free to blame that former government, call it traitorous, and demanded abrogation of the treaty.

The great depression of the early 1930s affected Battenberg just like it affected the rest of Germany, which had over six million unemployed. That was a staggering unemployment rate of more than 37%. As was the case in the rest of Germany, in Battenberg, farmers could not make ends meet, were deeply in debt, and were in danger of losing their farms. Throughout Germany, the middle class had lost their savings in the 1920s inflation, which had only recently ebbed, and the industrialists feared a Bolshevik revolution. The Weimar government was paralyzed by not being able to command a majority in the Reichstag. Hitler took advantage of the problems in Germany by giving charismatic speeches that promised what most people wanted to hear. "What is there to loose?" was a common expression. So his ranks grew. In Battenberg, the unemployed factory workers and the indebted farmers made up the largest part of the early S.A. membership. My father's business was affected by the absence of these party members as customers, but being an optimist, he interpreted this as a beneficial result since they were the former customers who had trouble paying their bills, and thus their absence was not a catastrophic loss.

Once Hitler took control of the government he resolved the problems by implementing his National Socialist policies. He started a tremendous rearmament program, enlarged the army, built superhighways (autobahns) enabling rapid transit of troops, threw Jews out of government jobs, making room for Aryans, built public works projects, and reduced the women's roll in the work force so that they could concentrate on housekeeping and childbearing. Within three years, unemployment had been reduced from six million to one million. No wonder they liked him. Few cared that trade unions had been abolished and replaced by a single National Socialist Labor Party or that Jews lost their jobs. Likewise, restrictions such as getting permission to change jobs and not being allowed to strike were accepted as the price of increased employment. By controlling the press and radio and arresting the Communist leaders and trade union leaders, Hitler silenced any effective remaining opposition.

As for the farmers, Hitler made it unlawful for any farmer to be removed from his land because of debt. Conversely, he made it unlawful for any farmer to sell or leave his land. Farmers were idealized. Supported by sentimental propaganda, farmers were acclaimed the salt of the earth, *Blut und Boden* (blood and the soil). Furthermore, young non-farm and urban men age eighteen, prior to their army service, were inducted into the *Arbeitsdienst* to work in rural areas, while women that age were expected to contribute one year of service on the farms (*land jahr*). That gave many farmers cheap help. No wonder that the farmers who obtained free help cheered the Führer. An Arbeitsdienst encampment was located on the outskirts of Battenberg. I often watched their formations, in gray uniforms and shovels carried like rifles, singing as they marching to work on the local farms or farm-related projects.

To insure long-term acceptance of the racial, political, and social policies, the Nazis organized the German youth. German Aryan boys had to join the Hitler Youth, where they were indoctrinated into Nazi political beliefs. The Hitler Youth was not only a recreational and social club, it was a compulsory way of life. Aside from a blood oath of allegiance to "Hitler, the savior of our country," they were obligated to educate their parents and report any dissension so that "help" could be brought to bear. Many parents became afraid to speak their mind for fear of being reported by their children.

Freedom of speech and secret ballots were not part of German life. I recall an incident that took place during November 1933. On that date there was a national election of a single party slate. Of course by the time this election took place, Jews no longer voted. The ballot gave a choice of YES or NO for the Nazi party and the vote was overwhelmingly, over 95 percent, in favor of the party. In Battenberg, there was only one voter who did not vote for the Nazi party. That vote was cast by a tailor (*Schneidermeister*) named Schmitt. That evening there was a torch-light victory parade organized and led by the local S.A. leader Jakob Rudolph. I recall watching it as it passed our house. At the front of the parade was the taunted tailor Schmitt with a very large placard strung around his neck with the message *Schneidermeister Schmitt ist ein Volksverräter* (tailor master Schmitt is a national traitor). It was vivid experiences like this that sooner rather than later caused Battenbergers to conclude that in their self interest they better toe the line of national unity, and give Hitler a chance to implement his plan for a new greater Germany. There may have been objectors and specific objections, but there appeared to be general satisfaction, yes even great happiness with Hitler in Battenberg's non-Jewish population.

Chapter 4

The Hitler Impact Grows

Frau Ruppel was angry. Most of her students could sense that immediately. Her normally friendly demeanor was strained. Her normally floating gait was choppy, and most telling of all, she snapped at any remark anyone made. Usually she hid her inner emotions from the students, but not now. This time she would obey "orders" from the Hauptlehrer Kolb, but not without showing the world that she disagreed with them. The orders were for the first of what were to become regular school assemblies, of military-like formation in straight rows and columns of all students, class by class, aligned in three blocks around the flagpole in the school courtyard. Jewish students were not to be allowed to participate in the assembly, and were to stand in a group by themselves, at a substantial distance behind the massed students.

This first assembly was in honor of Hitler's birthday, and Herr Bachman, who taught the fifth and six grades, announced in a loud and clear voice, "We celebrate this birthday of our great leader and Reich-chancellor Adolf Hitler by pledging to him no less than our sacred lives. We herewith swear eternal allegiance to him and destruction to all who are not in sympathy with his holy battle. We raise our right arm as a symbol of our oath. Repeat after me three times: *Sieg Heil! Sieg Heil! Sieg Heil* (hail to our victory)!" All students raised their right arms and repeated each of the three Sieg Heils in unison after Herr Bachman. Then the new swastika flag was ceremoniously raised while the students sang the two national anthems. The first was the new Nazi anthem that had just recently been taught.

Die Fahne hoch. Die Reihen fest geschlossen...

Raise the flag
Close the ranks
S.A. marches
in solitary steps.
Comrades who were shot
by the Red front reactionaries
march with us in spirit...

Then what had been Germany's national anthem long before:

Deutschland Deutschland über alles
Über alles in der Welt...

Germany, Germany above everything
above everything in the world...

I was anxious to join in this moving experience, and so I and our little group started to sing. Immediately, a senior student ran over to us and said, "Herr Kolb forbids you to sing. It is verboten for Jews to sing our sacred songs." I was scared and shocked and started to cry.

So there we stood, very uncomfortably, the five Jewish students of Battenberg: my sister Inge, her classmate Gretel Stern, Hannelore Stern, who was my classmate and Gretel's sister, I, and the youngest in the group, Gisela Eckstein, my second cousin.

Frau Ruppel felt that this treatment was unfair but was told by Hauptlehrer Kolb that the choice was obedience or dismissal. She tried as best she could to console us. Fortunately, the younger three students were in her classes so for us the aftermath of the morning's event was somewhat eased. After school, when Inge and I returned home, we could not control our emotions. We cried as we related the embarrassing event to our parents. Mother tried to console us with the proverb: "Sticks and stones will break my bones but words can never hurt us." Father was not as ready to accept the unfortunate event and decided to have a talk with Frau Ruppel and Herr Kolb. He did so, but without success. The orders received by the school were more emphatic than usual. All the teachers could do was express their sympathy and assure my father that these directives would not diminish their efforts to give us a good education. They also confided that Herr Bachman was an active member of the Nazi party[3] and insisted on strict compliance with orders from above.

Little by little the camaraderie my father had shared with the majority of the war veterans of Battenberg evaporated. The pressures not only of the Nazi party members but also the pressure from children became a moving force that gradually isolated us. People became afraid of the consequences of associating publicly with Jews, any Jews. Games of skat (a card game) that my father had played for many years with *Oberförster* (chief forest ranger) Theodor Schulz, butcher Fritz Seipp, hotel owner Karl Clemens and barber Fritz Stinzing were canceled for one excuse after another. They were still politely friendly but things just were not the same. For

---

[3] In later years, Frau Ruppel too joined the Nazi Party and eventually received the prestigious gold party pin for superior adherence to the Nazi dogma.

example, butcher Seipp suggested to my mother: "Don't come here to buy. I'll bring you whatever you need. Just call your orders in by telephone. I've talked to the switchboard operator, and she understands!"

You see, in Battenberg only business people had telephones. My father was one of the first to get a telephone, and our telephone number was 7, just 7. An operator made all phone connections on a manual switchboard at the post office. To make a phone call, you picked up the receiver and hand-cranked the magneto until you heard the voice of the operator. You then told her whom you wished to speak with. She then pushed the button that rang the destination. When that phone was picked up, she connected the two circuits and conversation between the two parties took place. The switchboard had about 100 connections, several of which connected to the nearby city of Frankenberg. Since Frankenberg was connected to other cities, long distance calls could be arranged. In Battenberg, telephone service was only available when the switchboard was manned, from 8 AM to 8 PM weekdays. Sunday phone service was from 8 to 9:30 AM and 12 to 1 PM. There were less than 80 telephones in all of Battenberg.

Barber Stinzing, the men's and women's barber as well as druggist and tobacco dealer, had regularly cut our hair. After several incidents where customers objected to sitting in the seats previously occupied by Jews, he suggested that we come to his shop after normal hours. My father refused such indignity and thereafter took us to a barber in a nearby village where no one knew us. I was too young to recognize my father's feelings, but now I can well imagine how painful it must have been for him to be so rejected by one of his close friends and army comrades. By now it was no longer just the distant government that practiced this completely unjustified anti-Semitism, the local people were infected with this poison. The clouds had darkened.

Life became progressively more difficult in Battenberg. One of the incidents that upset me related to events that may seem hard to comprehend today. In Battenberg, cows and horses were used as draft animals to pull farmers' wagons. As the animals pulled their loads along the streets, they often defecated. This was especially true in front of our house, which faced an uphill street. As the animals were urged to pull harder to maintain their pace pulling up the hill, the wagon drivers cracked their whips. This made the animals become more nervous, causing them to defecate more readily.

Cow dung and horse manure were valued for fertilizer for the gardens. Most six- to eight-year-old boys had homemade two-wheeled carts and short shovels for collecting draft animal droppings. Few droppings remained on the streets more than an hour after school let out. I was frequently more successful than other boys because of the inclined road in front of our house. I could rush out as soon as I changed my school clothes for play clothes and was the first out on the street. One day, however, several slightly older boys ganged up on me, threw my own collection at me and warned me never to pick up droppings again. "Jews are not allowed to pick up droppings from Aryan horses and cows," was their dictum. When I came home, splattered with soft cow dung, Mother first thought that I was in an accident. When she heard my tale of woe, she tried to comfort me by explaining that none of the horses and cows were Aryan but that we really had enough fertilizer and it might be best that I engage in other activities.

Another incident occurred a little later across the street from our house in the small triangular park adjacent to the scene of the book burning. This park contained an impressive monument to the soldiers who had perished in past wars. It also contained a circular fountain with a statue of Hansel and Gretel carrying an umbrella from which water poured over the umbrella and back into the pool. The park had several benches and lush planting and was surrounded by a fence with a gate on the Marburger Street side.

Picnic, Battenberg, 1936
Right: Mr. and Mrs. Eckstein. Left: Mrs. Drucker.
Center: Inge.

Picnic, Battenberg, 1936
Upper left: Mr. Drucker, Mr. Stern, Mr. Eckstein, Gretel,
Father, Inge. Seated: Gisela, Hannelore, Norbert, Werner.

In 1934, a bright red flat-fronted kiosk was built in the park directly adjacent to the entrance gate. Here the Nazi party posted the current copy of the national weekly newspaper, *Der Stürmer (The Storm Trooper)*. This was not a conventional newspaper but an extremely bigoted propaganda rag headlining extreme atrocities allegedly committed by the Jews. The articles were based on absurd lies prepared under the supervision of the extreme anti-Semite Julius Streicher and of Hitler's propaganda chief Göbbels. At the bottom of the front page in large letters was the slogan "The Jews are our misfortune." One edition contained images and stories of Jews killing Christian babies for their blood. Once when this libelous material was displayed at the kiosk, several older boys from my immediate neighborhood, who formerly had played with me, coaxed and forced me to accompany them to the kiosk and read "the truth about the Jews." I could barely read, so they prompted me and intimidated and pummeled me to the point where I cried and apologized that I did not do it! Dark clouds indeed. I was so embarrassed by this incident that I never told my parents. My embarrassment was not only because of the subject matter of *Der Stürmer*, but because boys who I thought were still casual friends turned so uncomfortably against me.

To compensate for the lack of social interaction, the Jewish families of Battenberg turned to each other. They were friends before Hitler came to power, but now these casual friendships deepened. Our closest friends were the Leo and Henriette Stern family. My constant companion was their daughter, my classmate, Hannelore. My sister Inge played with their older daughter Gretel. We spent much time in their house and they in ours. Lotti and Emi Schneider, our neighbors, were still friends but in a visibly diminished manner. Before long we hardly ever played together. Then there were Gisela and Norbert, the children of my father's second cousin Berta and Berthold Eckstein. Gisela was a year or so younger than I was;

Norbert was even younger. Gisela played with us, but when Norbert tagged along his relative immaturity led us to ostracize him. Berta was often upset about our apparent snobbishness.

Another "too young" playmate was Hans Isenberg, whose parents lived at the far end of Hauptstrasse. His grandfather, Sigmund, visited us regularly with Hans in tow to pick up potato peels, fresh-cut grass, and other scraps suitable for feeding his cattle. Cattle dealers always found food scraps handy as these diminished the cost of maintaining their transient cattle herd. Most of the time they held only two or three cows. With the Hitler enthusiasm on the rise, trading by Jewish cattle dealers became more and more difficult. Sigmund optimistically repeated the opinion shared by most Jewish cattle dealers that "No matter what Hitler's edicts might be, German farmers could not prosper, nay, survive without the cattle dealers, and lo and behold, the cattle dealers were almost exclusively Jewish." How wrong they were. Within a year all Jewish cattle dealers, and there were thousands of them, were all unemployed.

Besides these Jewish families, there was the Herman Drucker family. They had no children our age. Then there were the Jewish families residing in Battenfeld, Allendorf and Laisa. These were the neighboring villages each with a few Jewish families, all of whom were members of the Jewish congregation. Our congregational synagogue was located in Battenfeld. The villages were each two or three miles apart. This was considered to be within walking distance, especially so on Saturday mornings. Saturday morning religious service became a focal point for socializing. After services, most congregants jaunted to the home of Rosalie and Herman Oppenheimer, just a few houses away from the synagogue. Here schnapps was offered to the men, and each child received one sprinkle-covered chocolate candy, a nonpareil. Herman Oppenheimer was my grandmother Rossetta's brother. Rosalie was the daughter of the old Mr. Drucker.

All the congregational families were related, though some were more distantly related than others. When all the male adults attended services, they numbered perhaps fifteen to twenty. With children and a few women, services may have had up to thirty attendees.

The synagogue consisted of a one-room building about 30 feet by 40 feet with a balcony on three sides. That is where the women sat, talked, and sometimes prayed. Men were positioned around the perimeter of the lower floor and faced towards the center where there was a platform called the *bema* on which the Torahs[4] were read. The Torahs were kept in an ornately carved wooden cabinet, the ark, at the east end of the room. Each Torah scroll was tied together in the rolled-up mode with a *wimpel*, a linen cloth less than a foot wide and about five feet long. Each wimpel was dedicated to a local Jewish newborn male and had the name of the Jewish boy as well as proverbs and blessings embroidered on it with colorful silk threads. Each Saturday when the congregation members took a Torah from the ark to read a portion thereof, the children were given the wimpel to roll up tightly in preparation for its future reuse. Wimpels of attending boys were rotated for reuse after the torah reading. The greatest joy was to have your wimpel appear. I could recognize mine the moment the torah was untied. Since there were only a few boys in the congregation my wimpel appeared quite frequently. I still have fond recollections of these uplifting occasions.

To conduct religious services, the congregation had a *Vorbeter*, a leader of services who was technically hired by the state. He also taught Hebrew school and served as cantor and rabbi. We knew him respectfully as *Lehrer* (teacher) Amsterdam. He had a wife and four children. As a supplement to his meager salary, he lived in a rent-free house directly adjacent to the synagogue. The house had an attached classroom where we

---

[4] Torah is a large handwritten scroll containing the first five books of the bible (the Pentateuch).

attended Hebrew school. Even though he had a free home and a government stipend, Herr Amsterdam had a hard time making ends meet.

Each week, during religious services, a portion of the Torah is read. For this reading, seven men are honored by being sequentially called to bear witnesses. At our synagogue, whenever a man was called to be a witness to the reading of the Torah, the custom was to make a pledge for a donation, which was called *schnoder*, to the congregational fund. Unless there was a special occasion, donations generally were two to three marks, the equivalent of fifty to seventy five cents American currency. Whenever a male relative came to visit and attend religious services he was certain to be given the honor to be a witness. Then everyone awaited the announcement of his donation. I recall Uncle Salli's visit when he donated 100 marks. For weeks the post-service conversation at Oppenheimer's revolved around Salli's largess.

A not so pleasant memory was the Jewish New Year high holiday service in the fall of 1935. The policeman from Battenfeld had been ordered to sit in the back of the synagogue and to listen to the sermon by Herr Amsterdam, ostensibly to make sure that there would be no anti-Nazi statements in his sermon. The policeman's presence very much intimidated Herr Amsterdam so that he became all mixed up when he tried to deliver his sermon. Some of the women started to cry, and we children did not know what to do. We were probably on our best behavior during that service.

Even though he was born and raised in Poland, Herr Amsterdam spoke perfect German. He had come to Germany to study to become a rabbi, but found limited opportunity to obtain such a position. Recognizing this limitation and in dire financial need, he left the seminary to take the post in Battenfeld. At least here he had a rent-free home and an income, though that was very limited. Despite financial hardship, these were to be his golden times.

In Battenberg we tried to adapt to life as it evolved. When in 1935 the news that the Saar district was returning from French to German jurisdiction, there was a national celebration. A special commemorative stamp was issued. When cousin Hans and his family came from Korbach to visit that Sunday, he taught me a new song:

Deutsch ist die Saar.
Deutsch immer da.

German is the Saar.
German for evermore.

We children wanted to be part of the celebration, but that night after the Löwensterns went back to Korbach, we experienced our window being broken for the first time by stones thrown by teenagers in the Hitler Youth. This event took place after a celebratory torch-light parade by the Hitler Youth. They shouted slurs and sang anti-Semitic songs as they loitered around our house and in the nearby park. Then suddenly we heard the nerve-shattering sound of breaking glass. A few more epithets and then they dispersed. Our family was extremely upset as we picked up the glass shards from all over the floor and the beds and carefully removed the remaining sharp-edged pieces of glass from the window frames. I remember my mother trying to hold back her sobs while my father was as stern in demeanor as I ever saw him. Inge and I were almost too scared to cry, but cry and sob we did, yet tried to be as good as we knew how and very gingerly helped with the cleanup.

Such vandalism occurred thereafter with increasing frequency. My father's attempt to have the police act met with no success. Before long, at night, whenever there were these taunting shouts on the street below, we all gathered in the second floor center hall to avoid getting hurt by flying glass.

Such stone throwing occurred more than a dozen times while we remained in Battenberg. Each time, we'd first hear shouts, threats and taunts by a gang of youth and a sprinkling of adults loitering in front of our house and in our open side courtyard. Sometimes they chanted some anti-Semitic slogans in unison, then cacophonous sounds, laughter and then stones. First one or two and then a fusillade of stones were aimed at the second floor windows of our bedrooms and living room. Often the initial stones just hit the glass and bounced back. Then before long a window pane crashed to the floor, shattered, and was followed by a cacophony of shattering glass as more and more stones hit their target. After perhaps throwing 50 stones in five to six minutes, the bombardment ceased and we heard the crowd disperse. First my father and shortly thereafter my mother inspected the damage. The first few times it happened, Inge and I cried and were consoled by Oma (Rosetta), who reassured us that she would see to it that the hoodlums, whom she called *Lumpen* (rags), would be punished. Eventually Inge and I became more hardened and immediately helped clean up the shards and kept looking for ever smaller pieces of glass. Our reward and consolation often was the invitation to join our parents in their beds, which we happily accepted. There was a wonderful feeling of comfort and security in snuggling up with our parents. Though they may not have returned to sleep, I did fall asleep soon after I felt the warmth of their bodies and their comforting embrace.

One morning after such an event, when my father unlocked the front door to the store, the door knob, lock and the front stoop were covered with dog excrement. Frustrated to the hilt, my father then reluctantly started to surrender to the conviction held by many other Jews that "remaining in Battenberg and in Germany, for that matter, was not realistic." That meant selling the store and emigrating from Germany. The United States was apparently the most feasible destination. Palestine was another option, but there were disturbing reports of fighting between Arabs and Jews. Most European countries didn't want immigrants and wouldn't let immigrants work because there was not enough work for their own citizens. And in America there was Aunt Lene. America seemed to be the choice of many other Jewish families that were considering or actually leaving Germany.

The thought of leaving Battenberg was very painful for my father since he considered himself so much a part of life there. This was where his roots were. His forefathers had lived there for over two hundred years. His son was named in honor of the founder of Battenberg, the Earl Werner, who lived in the thirteenth century. This was the land he loved. This was the country and the town for which he fought and was wounded. This was where his comrades in arms resided, even if at the moment they were being intimidated by the Nazi regime. True, the German children were being poisoned against him and other Jews, but a new government could reverse this policy quickly. On the other hand, making a living was becoming almost impossible, and the pain of being treated like an outcast was becoming unbearable.

Doubts about leaving, however, arose every time any expression of support occurred. For example, the streets of Battenberg were quite clean since hardly anyone dropped paper or other litter; however, to keep the streets immaculate, there was an elderly couple, Herr and Frau Feisel, who lived at the edge of dignified poverty. They earned a small salary from the town by manually sweeping the streets with their handmade brooms. They earned a little extra money by trapping moles, which paid a bounty of ten *Pfennig*, the equivalent of about three American cents each. Frequently, Frau Feisel came into my father's store bedecked with a necklace of recently trapped moles. She was anti-Nazi and urged my father to resist the pressures just as she and her husband tried to do on every possible occasion.

Another example of support was shown by Hermine Beil, neighbor of the local tin smith, who continued to shop at my father's store and also came to our home with butter cookies and encouragement not to give up the fight. She shared our family's love of nature and of the lands around Battenberg and repeatedly expressed her view that the balance of nature was against the dictator.

Other people also expressed their support, but all this did not suffice to convince my father. Although wavering back and forth, he gradually came to accept the reality that Jews in Germany were not only losing their equal status but were becoming more and more ostracized.

Even then, the thought that Jews would be exterminated, yes killed, in an organized plan did not enter my parents' minds. To boot, letters from Lene in America emphasized the extent to which the Depression was making it very difficult to earn a living there. Palestine, the other alternative, was being subjected to bloody riots by Arabs who constituted the vast majority in that part of the world. There seemed to be no easy solution to the frightful problems at hand. Oh, how the clouds had really darkened.

Discussion of these problems was continuous whenever my father and his brothers-in-law got together. They did this more and more frequently. On many weekends, either we traveled to Korbach, or Sigmund or Julius or both visited us with their families.

On one occasion, while driving to Korbach by automobile, we traveled through a village (I believe it was the village of Thalitter) and saw along the road a life-sized effigy of two elderly Jews. They had very exaggerated features, ugly faces with hooked noses and hunched backs. The man had a cane with a small bag draped over his shoulder. The woman had glasses and a walking stick. Behind them, attached to a stone wall, was a directional sign *Zu Palestina*. In front of them was a large panel upon which was written a derogatory poem. My father stopped the car to take a hasty picture of that scene. I still have a faded copy of that photograph and tried to decipher the words. They run something like this:

O HERR GIB UNS DEN MOSES WIEDER
AUF DAS ER SEINE GLAUBENSGLIEDER
GEFÜRE INS GELOBTE LAND.
NOCH EINMAHL LASS DAS MEER SICH TEILEN.
LASS DIESE ROTE WASSERSCHEIDE
ENFANGEN DIE WIE DAS ERSTE MAHL
UND WENN NUN IN DER MEERESMITTE
DIE GANZE JUDENSHAFT IST DRINNEN
O HERR DAN MACH DIE KLAPPE ZU
UND ALLE VÖLKER HABEN RUHE

Translated it reads something like this:

O Lord give us Moses one more time
so that he can take his fellow believers
and lead them to the promised land.
Once more let the ocean part.
Let this Red Sea's separation
receive them just as previously
and when in the middle of the sea
the entire Jewish clan is there
O Lord then close the trap
and all countries will have peace.

Chapter 5

My Father's Demise

The reality of blatant anti-Semitism affected all members of our family.

It had not only crept into Battenberg, but had spread throughout Germany.

The typical German Jewish predicament was thus: The family had in past generations existed with one bread winner, the man of the house. Now for reasons beyond his control, he loses his job without any possibility to regain his means of livelihood.

Else's husband, Dr. Moritz Elias (Uncle Mor) was no longer permitted to treat non-Jewish patients who participated in the Social Security system. That edict, which applied to all German Jewish doctors, eliminated about 90 percent of his patients. His practice shattered, he regretfully realized he could no longer continue life as a doctor in Germany and decided to emigrate to the United States as soon as possible. At that time, Jewish emigration from Germany to the United States was not as difficult as it would soon become since the annual quota established by the United States for immigrants from Germany was only slightly smaller than the number of qualified applicants. He could get a visa provided that he had a sponsor in the United States who would set aside funds to assure that he and his family would not become a burden to the government. His sister-in-law, Lene Simon (Aunt Lene), who had emigrated to the United States in 1924, came to the rescue by producing an affidavit of five hundred dollars. This was the escrow fund required by the immigration service. In those days, five hundred dollars was enough to feed a family for about one year.

Uncle Mor also had a good friend and fellow doctor who had recently emigrated to the United States from Germany for the same reason. He urged Mor to come to the city of Utica in upstate New York where he would help Mor obtain his American medical license. And so, in 1935, after a visit to Battenberg to say good-bye, the Elias family—Else, baby Hans Marcus, and Moritz—sailed for America. Oma was very upset for she could not comprehend that another of her daughters would leave her forever.

Mor was smart and lucky. Within a very short time after arriving in America, he passed the then rather stringent English and physician's examinations and obtained a license to practice medicine. He settled in as family practitioner near Utica in a factory town called New York Mills.

Less than a year later, Julius Löwenstern, sent a plea to Lene to do likewise for him and his family. At first Lene responded with a litany of the tough circumstances facing people in the Depression-raked USA. He would not have an easy time obtaining a job, and no one needed salesmen who could not speak English. This negative response very much disturbed and discouraged the Löwensterns. When, at the next family gathering, the letter from Lene came up, my father wrote a strong letter back to her, explaining that the circumstances had become dire. He wrote that the earlier expectation of Hitler's being deposed from power was no longer realistic. He also encouraged Herta and Julius not to weaken in their resolve and to continue to press Lene for an affidavit.

Nathan and Lene Simon did manage to put another $500 in escrow, although this was a very substantial part of their assets. Additionally they had to consider the plight of Nathan's brother Louie and his family who were also trying to get out of Germany and who likewise depended on them to get to America.

Three funds of $500 each—a total of $1500—added up to a very substantial sum. In the mid-1930s, the earning power and the cost of things were very different from today. A factory worker considered himself well paid if he earned $30 per week. That was 75 cents an hour. On the other hand, a two-bedroom apartment in New York City was easily rented for $30 per month. Bread cost 8 cents per loaf and milk 10 cents per quart. $15 could buy a suit, and movie admission was 25 cents (for a double feature). So $500 dollars represented more wealth than many people had.

Salli, my father's younger brother who practiced dentistry in Hamburg, encountered the same fate as his brother-in-law Mor. Salli was still a bachelor and had several friends in England, and thus arranged to emigrate to England where dentists were in short supply. Therefore it was not too difficult for him to get working papers. Because of substantial unemployment in England and most other countries, immigrants in general could not obtain authorization to take paying jobs. Since the United States did not have these restrictions, the solution for most German Jews was to go to the United States. The United States, however, had severe restrictions on the number of immigrants allowed from each country in the form of quotas. If too many people from one country wanted to enter the United States, they would each have to get a quota number and wait their turn. That soon became the situation for German emigrants.

At about the same time, Marga, Nanny and Sigmund's oldest daughter who was by now in her early twenties, expressed a strong desire to go to Palestine where a close male friend of hers had recently gone. Sigmund saw this as an opportunity to get some of his money out of Germany and to get Marga to a safer place. After much deliberation, he and Nanny acceded to her wishes.

I remember one detail in particular of Marga's farewell visit to Battenberg. Normally when we ate bread for breakfast, we put either butter or jelly on the bread, but not both. Mother would say, "We don't own two houses so we don't cover our bread with two spreads." Marga, however, was quite meticulous in covering every part of her bread with butter and then, with the same meticulous care, added jelly to the bread, making sure that no part of the bread was without both. I was sure that Marga had at least two houses since that would be the only way a double spread would be possible.

Marga was warm and friendly. She was tall and slender and extremely attractive—and she knew it—and seemed also to be condescendingly sophisticated. In the company of us children she considered herself an adult. Ilse, her sister who was six years younger, was much more down to earth and was always a fun companion for my sister and me to be around. Sigmund and Nanny were the oldest of my father's kin and also the wealthiest. They felt they might be able to live out their lives in Germany even if they could not continue to operate their store. They planned and later executed the sale of their store and then moved to Frankfurt where they expected to enjoy anonymity. They lived in a modest fifth floor walk-up apartment in a decent neighborhood not far from the opera house. Here they felt they had found the security they desired.

By the time the Löwensterns emigrated to the United States, my father and mother had established a plan of action for our family. My father would enroll in a special school where he would take expedited training to become a baker. Once he graduated, he would emigrate to America, establish himself, and then send for the rest of the family to join him. Bakers were in reasonable demand in America and this would permit him to earn a living much more quickly than emigrating as a merchant. The idea of his becoming a mechanic, a trade much closer to his inherent skills, apparently was never seriously considered.

To implement this plan, my father needed an immigration quota number. The U.S. permitted only 27,300 immigrants from Austria and Germany to enter each year. Since the number of German Jews wanting to emigrate exceeded the quota, numbers were issued and prospective immigrants had to wait until their number was called.

At the rate the numbers were called, it was estimated to take a year or more for our number to be called. Although that may seem a long time, at the time of application there appeared to be no imminent mortal danger. The worst that Jews anticipated was that the harassment would increase and that earning a living would become near impossible. We would have to live solely from savings and the sale of assets until we could leave Germany.

The priorities now were to sell the store and house, take the baker's training and learn the English language.

Because of Nazi regulations, the house and store could only be sold to "qualified" Nazi party members at a price to be approved by the Nazi party. In case of multiple interested buyers, preference was to be given to the party member of longest or highest standing. No one in Battenberg was qualified to buy the business, so my father placed an advertisement in a trade paper specializing in sales of Jewish-owned enterprises. This resulted in the sale to a Mister Paul Hoff. He was a young man in his early thirties who had joined the Nazi party about ten years earlier, in 1926, when he was looking unsuccessfully for a job. Since party membership was relatively small in those years, he had a membership number that was very low and thus extremely favorable in terms of party recognition.

Mister Hoff was short but athletic looking and was a shrewd opportunist. He realized that he did not have the experience to operate the store efficiently on his own, so he offered to have my father help him for a little while. He agreed that our family could live upstairs for two years or until we emigrated. Mister Hoff was single but had a female friend whom he planned to marry as soon as the store purchase was completed. He would live on the main floor, thus giving us substantial privacy.

The house, the land, the store and the inventory all together sold for 5,000 Deutschmark—the equivalent of about $1,250. My father had spent more than that just for the house addition. Since Mister Hoff had such a favorable party membership number, it was futile for my father to attempt to get another buyer. Mister Hoff told my father that this sum was the absolute maximum he would pay, but he'd give my father the opportunity to earn additional money for his help after the sale. This consisted primarily of repairing centrifuges and servicing established farm customers in the outlying villages. Since these villages had no resident Jews, they were less conscious of official anti-Semitism and more tolerant of my father working. Payments were made to my father out of the proceeds of the business. This included a commission for sales my father made to farmers in neighboring villages. This auxiliary income was not be recorded and thus was much like a bonus.

Since Mr. Hoff was single, from out of town, and not yet acquainted with the locals, he often came to visit us "upstairs" and in unguarded conversation revealed that he really did not believe in the Nazi party philosophy and had no ill feelings toward Jews like us, but that he loved the opportunity the Nazi party gave him to make a *Mensch* out of himself.

It must have been extremely painful for my father to surrender his hard-earned enterprise and see his means of income lost, but he never conveyed that disappointment to us, his children. After the sale, he continued to travel to nearby communities and came home early evenings, warmly greeting us and proudly calculating the commission he had earned from the sales of the day. These sums were not large but permitted him to maintain some vestige of self esteem.

By the summer of 1937, a year after the sale, with the escalation of Nazi anti-Semitic policies, my father's earnings were down to nothing. It must have been a tremendous mental strain on my parents to realize that our family would have to live on our limited assets as long as we remained in Germany. However, I recall no incident whatsoever that would have given me a hint of my parents' concern. My mother and father were only drawn together more tightly by circumstances and always conveyed a feeling of family unity, of affection and compassion to Inge and me. Our life was still bearable. And to top it off, Oma, our grandmother who shared our home most of the time, truly doted upon us. Oma had her own little financial nest egg and had very few expenses except for traveling to visit her other children, an activity that diminished as they emigrated one by one. In 1937 she made an extended trip to Uncle Salli in England.

After the house and store were sold, the vandalism—primarily the breaking of windows—diminished for a while, but by the summer of 1937 it had increased again. My father was scheduled to start his training to become a baker right after the Jewish high holidays in mid-September. Before he left, he decided to do whatever he could to stop the violence to which we were subjected. Trouble most often occurred on weekend evenings after the Hitler Youth had their meetings. One evening he positioned himself next to a window facing the road, awaiting the action, which soon started. As usual, the uniform-clad teenage boys shouted and sang boisterously on the way home from their meeting. Typical of their songs: *"Wen das Judenblut vom Messer spritzed dan geht's noch mahl so gut"* (when the Jewish blood splashes from the knife then things will be twice as good). Then some shouts of *"Jud raus!"* (Jew get out!), and similar derogatory slogans. Next some stones flew, the first few often missing the windows, but still making a thud as they hit the wall. Eventually a stone hit its target. A window broke, accompanied with the piercing sound of glass hitting the floor. Laughter ensued from below. At that moment my father shone his high-powered flashlight at their faces trying to identify the culprits. This did not deter them. The next morning my father went to the police with the names of the perpetrators he had recognized and he asked to file a formal complaint. Most shocking to him was the observation of Rapplegeorge, amidst the Hitler Youth, as one of the stone throwers. He was evidently spurring them on if there was any need to do so. The very small police force in Battenberg was a state agency headed by one senior policeman. Father returned disillusioned; the policeman had explained to my father that although he personally disapproved of civil disorder, "those" actions were condoned by the "Party." He did, however, indicate that he'd give the matter further thought and see what he could do.

Several days later, the policeman came to our home and requested that my father accompany him to the police station where he would be taken into "protective custody" (*Schutzhaft*). The policeman did not say for how long, but my father had enough faith in him and the police policies to believe this could only be for a very short time. After all, schutzhaft was understood to be for his own protection. Apparently the publicity surrounding the recent incident had aroused some strongly hostile feelings towards us in the families my father had identified. My father's concept of obedience and the policeman's firm insistence led my father to submit to this camouflaged form of arrest. Mother nervously packed a few overnight items in a small briefcase, which my father clipped to the small luggage carrier behind the bicycle seat. The policeman and my father then bicycled off while Mother hugged Inge and me and tried to assure us that this was all for the better. Only many decades later did she confess to us how upset and forlorn she was at that moment. Her anxiety increased when she was deterred from visiting him and could not get a meaningful answer to her inquiry as to when he would be released or why he was being held. She was only told that this was for his own good, yet authority to release him was subject to higher authorities.

Father came home several days later. He complained that he did not feel well. Apparently that was the reason he was released. At Mother's urging he went to bed. The next day, Sunday, he still did not feel right. I do not recall his specific complaints, but they were sufficient to have Mother suggest that he stay in bed a bit longer since the following day was Rosh Hashanah.

Normally I went to Hebrew school on Sundays together with my sister and the other Jewish children from Battenberg. However, since I had a mild cold and the family's routine had been upset by the recent events, Mother suggested that I stay home. That more than pleased me, and I busied myself with my toys.

Shortly before noon, I heard my mother scream. I ran into their bedroom where she was slapping my father's face, seemingly trying to revive him from what appeared to me to be a deep sleep. He did not respond. My father was dead.

Mother finally rushed down the stairs to Mr. Hoff's quarters and called Doctor Winkler on the telephone. She came back up, supported by Mr. Hoff, and told me that the doctor would come as soon as possible. He had reminded her that he was not allowed to administer to Jews, but since he and Louie were army buddies he'd come. He came several hours later but it was too late.

Father had been in apparent good health prior to his arrest. We do not know what happened while he was in custody. The circumstances were such that Mother would or could not question any of that. She was just too upset. I did not fully understand the finality of death and tried, unsuccessfully, to console my mother. Mr. Hoff silently almost sveltely left to go back downstairs. A little later, when Inge came home from

Hebrew school, the upset rose like a tidal wave in a storm. I recall Mother tightly hugging Inge and me as the three of us sat there, crying. Our sad disposition was interrupted by Doctor Winkler's arrival. Without much of an examination, he filled out the death certificate, stating heart attack (*Hertzanfall*) as the cause of death. He stayed only briefly and we were again left alone in our grief.

Chapter 6

Frankfurt

The next thing I remember is my mother, between sobs and tears, instructing me to run up our street to tell the Ecksteins, Druckers and Isenbergs that my father had died. I believe that my sister was dispatched in the opposite direction to convey the message to the Sterns. These were the Jewish families currently in Battenberg. In the absence of our own telephone, this seemed to be the obvious way to communicate. Our former telephone was now part of Mr. Hoff's business, and to impose on him for such personal use was apparently inappropriate.

I did not fully realize then the long-range impact my father's death would have on our family. As I ran up the street I felt mixed emotions, partly a sad feeling that something bad had happened and partly an elated sensation—stimulation and excitement. I had become the messenger of significant startling news. I sensed that for the first time in my life I had to do something of importance. Before the day was over, the village's Jewish adults were in our home, as was Lehrer Amsterdam. He took me aside and rehearsed the reading of the *kadish* (prayer for the dead) with me.

I remember the women preparing food in the kitchen. Mrs. Isenberg was peeling potatoes; my sister said to me that the peels were being cut very thick. I knew that our potato peels were always donated to the Isenbergs for cattle feed. Hence, if the peels were thick, there would be more cattle feed but less potato for eating. With food in scarce supply, this bothered Inge and me. I recall an odor in the house that I had never smelled before. I associated it with death since my father's corpse was in the bedroom for two days of Rosh Hashanah. There was no undertaker available to the Jewish families in Battenberg.

The day after Rosh Hashanah was the day of the funeral. In Battenberg it was common for a funeral of a respected member of the community to be accompanied to the cemetery by the local band playing the "Funeral March" by Chopin. If the deceased was a war veteran then the music included the sentimentally sad song *"Ich had ein Kameraden, einen besseren findest du nicht—"* In English this means: "I had a comrade, a better one you can't find—"

No such honors were paid to my father. A black-draped hearse pulled by a black horse carried the coffin from our house to the cemetery, which was about four miles away on a hill on the far side of the neighboring village of Battenfeld. Mr. Amsterdam, Mother, Inge, and I walked immediately behind the hearse with perhaps twenty-five Jewish congregants and family members walking behind us. Everyone wore black. There was not a single non-Jewish person from Battenberg who joined the funeral procession.

As we slowly started the procession, a considerable number of Christian children and some grownups watched from the curb. We had walked but a short distance when I felt the sting of a pitched stone. The children were throwing small stones at our procession and taunting us, mimicking Jewish mannerisms: *"Nu ja! Vater ist gestorben, Mutter lebt noch."* (Oh yea! Father died, but Mother is still alive). Soon, this was repeated by an increasing chorus and accompanied by a storm of stones. No one seemed to try to stop them. We could do nothing except to keep walking. We eventually passed the last houses of the village and proceeded on the way to Battenfeld. It seemed like an interminable walk as we proceeded down the main road to Battenfeld and then through that village and up the long hill to the cemetery.

At the grave I haltingly read the kadish. I was shaking with tension, but I could not cry. I was guided to pitch three shovels of dirt onto the coffin after it was lowered into the grave. Few sounds are as heart-wrenching as the thud of the first dirt hitting the coffin below. After my token effort, the male mourners completely filled the grave with soil. This was the customary way of burial. Fortunately, Oma was in England visiting with Uncle Salli at this time. But, to add to our grief, Oma's brother, in Battenfeld, Herman Oppenheimer, died just a few days later.

To assist Mother and give her moral support, a cousin of hers from Frankfurt, Bina Hamburger, came to stay with us for a few weeks. I was sent with my wooden hand wagon to meet her at the railroad station. When the train arrived, I saw a single passenger get off the train, a chic, well-coiffured woman dressed in black. She looked somewhat like my mother. I walked over to her and very hesitantly asked, *"Tante Bina?"*

She gave me a big hug and a thoughtful compliment, put her suitcase into my little wagon and said, "Please let me help you pull this home." The train station was at the bottom of the hill and I had entertained fears of not being able to pull it uphill with a load. Her offer was welcome.

Bina was a wonderful person—warm, positive, and full of fun. She made me feel like an important and knowledgeable person with her frequent questions. I usually was able to answer them and feel as though I was her guide and teacher. She was just the right support for Mother. Bina had a husband and a son in Frankfurt and was anxious to return to them once she felt that she could safely leave Mother alone. She and Mother spent much time discussing the immediate future, and Bina convinced

Mother to move to Frankfurt. It did not take much persuasion since conditions in Battenberg had reached such a low. As soon as the arrangements were complete, we left Battenberg and moved into a two-bedroom apartment on the first floor of 47 Mainzer Landstrasse in the western part of Frankfurt.

Frankfurt seemed like a new world to me. I was enrolled in the Philantropin, an all-Jewish school. It had separate rooms for each grade, unlike the combined grades at the school in Battenberg. It included a high school and had a large sports field a short distance away. Since the school was in the eastern part of Frankfurt, I rode my bicycle to and from school because taking the streetcar every day was too expensive.

The Stahls had already moved to Frankfurt, to an apartment not too far from us. Ilse visited us the day we moved in. She helped Mother unpack and spouted oodles of useful trivia that might aid us in our new home. She also told us of the Jewish clubhouse, the *Kultur Verein Haus* that was home to a number of Jewish organizations. There were clubs for all age groups. Ilse was an active member of a senior teen group. When Inge and I went with her a few days later, she enrolled me in the pre-teen age boys *Hashomer* Club and Inge in a similar girls club. The philosophy of the Hashomer Club was based on Zionism, the movement to establish a Jewish homeland in Palestine by peaceful means—by purchasing and settling on the land and living in peace with the neighboring Arabs. Another club was the Betar, whose members espoused a more aggressive approach to creating a homeland in Palestine. Often, we younger members listened to heated discussions by older members of the two groups as they debated their opposing philosophies.

Our club met once a week and planned activities for weekends both indoors and outdoors. Our leader, one of the senior teenagers, was thin but strong. We called him *Knoche* (bones). There were about twenty boys, all about my age, in our group. Our uniform was a white shirt and black or dark blue shorts. Periodically there were assemblies of several groups to view a special presentation or to make one. As I became enmeshed with Jewish people, I realized that there were more Jews in Frankfurt than there were people in Battenberg. That gave me a good feeling of confidence and self- esteem. I was no longer the oddball. For once there were boys, Jewish boys, my age to play with, and since local people did not know who I was, there was suddenly less fear of being mistreated. Non-Jewish boys of the neighborhood seemed to ignore me, and I did the same to them. Since we were new to the area, Mother, Inge and I benefitted from the anonymity offered by the big city.

I was anxious to become familiar with the city, so I decided to use my bicycle to do the exploring. I followed the streetcars running in front of our apartment to their terminals and then followed them back on my bicycle. Occasionally I became confused and got lost, but I would then wait for the next streetcar heading toward the desired destination and eventually get back to familiar territory. I did not tell Mother until after I returned since I knew she would not have permitted me to explore the city in this manner.

Frankfurt also seemed to be loaded with relatives. There were the Stahls and Bina and her family. Her son, Franz, was much older than I but was very friendly and took me to a number of places where I had never been to in my life. We went to the zoo, which was a real eye-opener. I had never been to a zoo and barely knew what a zoo was. Now I saw animals I had only seen pictured in books. Many I had never even heard of. I was continuously amazed, and Franz seemed to enjoy my thrill of discovery as much as I did. Another pleasurable occasion was when he took me to the "for Jews only" swim facility at the edge of the Main River. Here we played and swam and fooled around with complete freedom. I only then realized how restricted my life had been prior to moving to Frankfurt.

There was a cousin of my father, Leopold Fuld, and his wife, Liesel. He was in the diamond business. They had a grown son,

Hans, who had gone to South Africa to live with business friends. One glorious summer Sunday in 1938 Leopold invited Inge and me to one of the fanciest cafes in the elegant Zeil district in downtown Frankfurt. The café was owned by Jews and before the Hitler era was frequented by the aristocracy of Frankfurt. This was to be his treat for us. He ordered two wonderful servings of ice cream presented with wafer cookies, a fruit topping, and whipped cream. For himself, I believe he ordered a cup of coffee. The service was by waitresses in black dresses with white aprons and white crown-like headpieces. It was an elegance I had never experienced before. Leopold was a tall and stately man whose dignified posture was enhanced by his wearing a pince-nez[5] just like Franklin Roosevelt. The three of us sat on an elevated patio overlooking the pedestrian traffic. The elation, the sheer pleasure of such a luxurious environment, made a lasting impression on me. When we finished our ice cream and were trying to get the very last smidgen out with our spoons, he asked if we'd like another. We just could not say no, so he ordered second helpings. When we came home and told Mother—whom we now called "Mama"—of our good fortune, she expressed the feeling that we overstepped his hospitality and should be more moderate in future.

Frankfurt had a population of about thirty thousand Jews who had developed a solidarity among themselves, largely in defense of the isolation forced upon them by the Nazi protocols. Movies had signs in the ticket windows saying *Juden unerlaubt* (Jews not allowed). Most stores had signs in their windows: *Juden unerwünscht* (Jews not wanted). Such signs were located in most public facilities. Yet to me the summer of 1938 was like a new life. School, bicycling, swimming and playing with new friends all were pleasant experiences. Of course all my new friends were Jewish. I met some of them at the Hashomer Club

---

[5]Pince-nez are eyeglasses without connecting pieces to the ears. They are held in place by a spring that pinches the nose.

and others at school. Most of the boys I became friendly with lived in our neighborhood and had lived in Frankfurt all their lives, but several had migrated to this city from rural communities like mine. I reveled in the new experience of associating with boys my age who had no compunctions about playing with me. There were about six of us who became really close buddies. One friend taught me to play chess to the point of addiction, and later on when I left Frankfurt he gave me a present of a small portable chess set. I learned to play a fair game of ping pong at the Kultur Verein Haus where we spent many afternoons. Our mode of transportation was the ubiquitous bicycle, and sometimes we rode around as a group, just for the fun of it. That summer I had the first opportunity to exchange stamps with friends. Shortly after my father died, Mama had given me a stamp album that contained pictures of all the German stamps and room for future ones. It was the last present my father had bought for me.

My father's memory was with me frequently, especially when I was in my mother's presence. I could see that she mourned for him constantly, and tears welled in her eyes at the slightest reminder of him. I tried hard to console her but very often found myself crying with her.

At Mama's request I went to synagogue almost every Saturday to say kadish for my father. I attended the nearest large synagogue, the *Underlindau* Synagogue, which was a stately structure that could hold nearly one thousand worshipers and had a renown boy's choir. The cantor who performed most of the service had an operatic quality voice, and his harmony with the choir created an inspiring service. I was not only impressed with the service but awed by the synagogue structure itself. It had a high vaulted ceiling and was graced with several onion-shaped domes. The ornate interior and exterior architecture was in a style consistent with other major synagogues of Frankfurt and reflected a strong oriental influence. I initially went to this synagogue because

Uncle Sigmund offered to take me there with him. He was a member of that congregation. The boys' choir was led by my Philantropin music teacher, Herr Silverpfenig. One day at school, Herr Silverpfenig approached me with the proposition that he could almost guarantee me a grade of A in music if I would join the choir at the synagogue. I readily agreed and became probably the least qualified member of the choir. Unfortunately, the very select and well-known choir was rapidly deteriorating as one member after another left, emigrating from Germany with their parents. Herr Silverpfenig was very pleased with my good attendance record, though it was inspired by my urge to say kadish rather than my lust for singing.

Saturday afternoons Inge, Mama, and I took English lessons from a young man who had studied some English in college. The several marks he charged for one hour was one of the few expenses considered as important as food and rent. His limited knowledge of English permitted our vocabulary to grow very slowly and rather poorly. He primarily taught us words rather than sentences.

Anti-Semitism was all around us in Frankfurt and became part of our way of life. I had no personal contact with non-Jewish people except for the house janitor. His concern was only to keep the lobby spotless. The movie houses' signs "No Jews allowed" did not bother me since I was not accustomed to going to the movies. There had not been any movie theaters in or near Battenberg. Likewise the stores that had signs in their windows or on their doors stating that Jews were less than welcome did not affect me. I stayed clear of such places, so there were few confrontations. A few food items were rationed, and the allowances for Jews were smaller than for Aryans, but we managed. The radio and newspapers were full of anti-Semitic diatribe, but radios were not permitted to be owned by Jews, and newspapers were too expensive to be purchased every day. We thus had only limited exposure to local and national events.

Even with the limited exposure, the ever increasing anti-Semitic dictates somehow became quickly known to us.

It was not until October 1938 that my feeling of relative contentment was shattered. Our apartment was not far from the main railroad station. One evening in October we received unexpected visitors from Battenfeld. It was Herr Amsterdam with his wife and four children. They lugged several disheveled suitcases and bags and boxes. He told us that since he was technically not a German citizen but of Polish origin, he and his family were being evicted from Germany and ordered to return to Poland. It apparently made no difference that the children were born in Germany. They had taken the train from Battenfeld to Frankfurt where their connection to the train east would not depart until the next morning. They were virtually without funds and had only been given a few hours to leave Battenfeld. Mama prepared some food. We managed to clear enough floor space for them to sleep, and although our financial resources were limited, Herr Amsterdam gratefully accepted some money.

It was not until ten years later that Mr. Amsterdam visited us again in New York City and told us the rest of the story. When they arrived at the Polish border, together with many thousands of others, the Polish border guards would not let them in, and the German soldiers would not let them return. It was raining and there was nowhere to go for shelter. The area they were in was a muddy field. It was getting dark. There was extreme panic and frustration as these poor souls were stuck in a muddy no-man's land. During the night, Herr Amsterdam and his family and a number of others somehow managed to get across the Polish border. They eventually continued to Russia, where they somehow were aided on their way to China and then to Shanghai. Here, they had permission to stay but had no means of making a living. His oldest daughter eventually earned some money by prostitution and ended up marrying a reasonably well-to-do Chinese man. After the war, an international aid society helped them immigrate to the United States and settle in Baltimore except for the oldest daughter, who remained in Shanghai.

Of course, we could not predict what would happen to Mr. Amsterdam that day in Frankfurt, but we knew that his future looked grim.

The thousands of Jews of Polish descent who were deported from Germany included a family named Grynszpan. Their son, living in Paris, heard of this cruel deportation, and extremely upset, he vented his anger and frustration by shooting and fatally wounding an official of the German Embassy, a man named Ernst von Rath. This provided the Nazis with a pretext to carry out a long-planned attack (a national pogrom) on German Jews. It took place over the course of two days—November 9 and 10—and came to be known as *Kristall Nacht.*

Following the shooting, the ferocity and abusiveness of German propaganda against the Jews had been increased daily. As November commenced, I went to school as usual, but the radical statements appearing in the newspapers and on the radio affected everyone's mood and conversation. Special meetings led by Germany's leading Jew-baiter, Joseph Goebbels, were announced for the S.A., the brown-shirted Nazi party organization.

On Wednesday, November 9, when I arrived at school, our homeroom teacher, Doctor Bick, talked to us briefly about the current situation. He pointed out that although the level of anti-Jewish actions in Frankfurt had been less violent than in other communities, nevertheless, nation-wide anti-Semitic propaganda had been stirred up so much by the Grynszpan event that the school administration anticipated possible negative repercussions. He pointed out that roaming groups of Nazi storm troopers were always, but especially now, to be avoided, because they were allowed to physically hurt Jews without being penalized. He reminded us that we should be proud to be Jews, the carriers of a tradition many thousands of years old.

However, he strongly suggested that we go home directly and stay out of the streets for a few days to avoid the possibility of any Nazis taking advantage of us. He told us there would be no school for the rest of the week and gave homework assignments and then dismissed class.

I did not understand the severity of the situation. I discussed the state of affairs with my classmates. Some were scared and shaken, but most of them felt like I did. I felt that the school administration was overreacting to rumors and propaganda, but I was not too unhappy with the prospect of not attending school for a little while. Since I had moved to Frankfurt, I had never been confronted by gangs of Nazis, but I had heard of a number of incidents were Jews, both young and old, had been assaulted while walking in the streets.

I got onto my bicycle and proceeded to ride home. On my way, several speeding open-bed trucks loaded with S.A. men passed by me. That was not an unusual sight, but it made me uncomfortable, especially after the admonition received just a little while ago at school. As I got a bit closer to home, I heard fire engine sirens. My curiosity, together with time on my hands, caused me to follow one. It stopped near a very large and ornate synagogue, the New Synagogue on Boern Platz. It was in flames, but the firemen who were already at the site were training their hoses on the adjacent buildings. They were dousing these buildings, apparently to avoid the fire from spreading. The fire fighters did not make any attempt to extinguish the fire at the burning synagogue. I watched for a little while, looking around for anyone I might know. There were many spectators, but no one I recognized. Neither did anyone seemed to recognize me. There were occasional cheers when the flames flared up. After watching this spectacle for a little while, I felt sufficiently uncomfortable to leave as inconspicuously as I came and proceeded to cycle home.

Mama had heard that the Germans were going to get even with the Jews for killing the German official. She decided that since our apartment was on the first floor facing the main street it would be prudent to go to the Stahls' apartment, which was in a "better" neighborhood and was located on the fourth floor. She definitely wanted to avoid a repeat of her experiences of broken glass in Battenberg. We started walking to the Stahls', but there were S.A. men everywhere, especially around the Jewish stores along our way. As we approached a Jewish café, we saw a number of people watching as S.A. men destroyed the establishment. The windows were broken and baked goods, tortes, cookies, cakes and display stands were all lying on the sidewalk, smashed beyond use. Several cases of eggs were also completely smashed with the broken egg yolks running in rivulets into the gutter along the street. This was especially shocking to me because eggs were scarce and were rationed. I recall commenting that this was such a waste. Why didn't they at least take the eggs and use them?

We crossed the street to a safe distance away from the action, but I could not keep my eyes off the scene. At the next corner, Mama made us turn into a side street, making a slight detour to avoid further sights of destruction such as we had just witnessed. As we hurried along, we saw several men, apparently Jewish, being led under protest to a bus. They were being severely pushed and maneuvered quite apparently against their will by S.A. men. Then I saw one of the men being hit repeatedly by several S.A. men. I started to shiver, but at Mama's urging we kept going.

We arrived at the Stahls' residence in a state of anxiety. The news on the Stahls' secretly owned radio seemed to suggest that Jewish men would soon experience the wrath of the German *Volk*. Ilse was at a friend's house and had not yet returned home.

In view of the rumors and the realities we had witnessed so far, Aunt Nanni and Mama urged Uncle Sigmund to go to the attic of the apartment house to hide, just in case. Sigmund very reluctantly put on his overcoat and took a newspaper and went upstairs. Several hours later he returned, complaining that it was uncomfortable and boring up there, and this whole fear complex seemed to him to be exaggerated. The women agreed to serve him some soup and a sandwich but insisted that he then go back up to the attic at least for the night.

Sigmund had just started to eat his soup when there was a powerful knock at the door. Nanni opened the door, and was confronted by two uniformed policemen and a man in civilian clothes. Policemen always had been very civil and so were these, yet there was a solemnity, a seriousness in their demeanor. One of the policemen asked for permission to enter, and without waiting for an answer all three men immediately stepped into the apartment and walked into the dining room where my uncle was sitting. The civilian, wearing a long, dark leather coat carried a briefcase and held a note pad in his hand. He glanced at it, and asked my uncle: "Are you the Jew, Sigmund Stahl?" Barely waiting for a reply he ordered that Sigmund accompany them.

Sigmund was startled. He asked just one word: "Why?" Without getting a response to his question, he was curtly told he could take a small suitcase of overnight clothing.

One of the policemen offered the answer by his remark: "This matter of registering all Jewish men will probably be completed in a day or two." Sigmund was apparently so shaken that he did not utter a word. Nanni, her eyes glassed over with tears, rushed to get Sigmund's coat and a nearby briefcase into which she shoved a few items while Mama quickly wrapped and included the sandwich he had as yet not eaten. Sigmund gave Nanni a brief kiss, waved hesitantly to Mama, Inge and me, and within a few minutes the four men were gone. Inge and I witnessed all this while we were sitting in the kitchen. I did not move an inch throughout this happening. I sat there transfixed and scared. After the door closed behind them, there were a few seconds of silence. Then Mama, though extremely upset, tried to comfort an even more upset Aunt Nanny by pointing out to her that police involvement was a good sign since it would insure propriety.

Later that evening, after Ilse returned and was apprised of the scary preceding events, Mama decided that she, Inge and I should return to our apartment to sleep. Ilse would do her best to soothe Nanni's emotional upset, and we had not brought anything for staying over. There also was no spare bedroom. Before we left, the women tried to convince themselves and each other that Sigmund would probably return home the next day. After all, he had done nothing wrong and surely the Frankfurt police, always a bastion of civility, would do nothing improper. Mama thought that now that it had become dark, it would be safe to walk home, and she was anxious to check if our apartment was intact. The walk, which took less than half an hour, was uneventful since we avoided the main streets as much as possible and walked mainly through residential side streets. When we did arrive in our apartment, it was indeed intact, but we were all exhausted. Although I was exhausted by the evening of anxieties, I had a very difficult time falling asleep. Whenever I dozed off, I was reawakened by dreams of S.A. men arresting people and fires out of control. Finally, shortly before midnight, I did fall asleep.

Chapter 7

Kristall Nacht Aftermath

It was shortly after midnight, just after I had fallen asleep, that I was awakened by being shaken by my sister, who was sobbing. As I wiped the sleep from my eyes, the first thing I noticed was unfamiliar noises emanating from the adjacent living room. I got out of bed to examine what the commotion was all about and was astonished to see my relatives. Here were my uncle Walter Schloss, brother of my mother, his wife, Clara, their son, my cousin, Gerd, and my grandmother, Oma Rosa, my mother's mother. At first I thought I was dreaming again, but then reality set in. Between tears and hugs, I soon learned what had happened. I knew that they all had lived in the village of Frahmersheim where my mother was born, but yesterday, November 9, the entire family as well as the few other Jewish families in Frahmersheim were ordered to go to the town hall for "their protection." Town hall was several houses down the same street. While they were forcibly held there, their house was plundered of absolutely everything portable—clothing, food, furniture, appliances, curtains. Late that afternoon they were escorted back to their house to see the shambles. They were in shock and disbelief at the sight of unbelievable destruction and the absence of absolutely everything that was in the house just a few hours ago. There were no suitcases and nothing worthwhile to put in them even if any had remained. With nothing but the clothing on their bodies, they were then loaded into an open truck and driven several miles to a spot on the main road to the town of Alzei. There they were unloaded and ordered on pain of death never to return to Frahmersheim. After recovering slightly from a state of panic, they walked to the railroad station at Alzei, trying hard not to look as disheveled and upset as they actually felt. Fortunately, Uncle Walter had enough cash in his pocket to buy train tickets from Alzei to Frankfurt for the four of them.

We lived only a few blocks from the main railroad station, so when they arrived in Frankfurt, they walked to our apartment, arriving at our door upset beyond words. They told us their tale of woe between outbursts of sobs and anger. I tried to play with Gerd, but he was too fatigued and upset, and before long he fell asleep. The adults talked until later that night, trying to determine what to do. Our apartment was much too small to permanently accommodate four more people, and there was not enough money on hand to try to rent an apartment for them, even if one could be found. After much discussion, the home of Clara's parents seemed the best solution. Was that home still intact? Was Clara's family all right? How could we reach them quickly? Early the next morning, Clara's parents were called using the public telephone exchange at the Frankfurt railroad station and a sympathetic non-Jewish neighbor of Clara's parents at the other end. After learning that conditions were reasonably safe there, the decision was made. As soon as possible Walter, his family, and Oma would leave for Allendorf an der Lumda, about 100 kilometers away, where Clara's parents lived. Clara's parents apparently had escaped any direct incident and still had their home, which was large enough to accommodate the four now-homeless souls. Mama went with them to the railroad station and paid for the tickets since Uncle Walter was just about out of cash. As an emergency measure, Mama gave them some money for clothing and to cover whatever other needs were sure to arise.

After tearful goodbyes, Mama decided to check if Sigmund had returned home. He had not, and by now it was noon of November 10. She summoned enough courage to go to the local police station to try to find out what was happening. A very civil police officer explained to her that all Jewish men in this part of Frankfurt were interned at the *Messehalle*—the industrial convention center—and that the internment was under the jurisdiction of the Gestapo, the dreaded secret police.

The Messehalle was not very far away. Encouraged by the reasonable treatment she received at the police station, she decided to walk to the messe halle to see or try to find out what was happening there. As she approached the area, she met an acquaintance who told her that the men were being kept busy washing and mopping the facility while awaiting transport. Transport buses were constantly arriving empty and leaving filled with men. She could see the buses coming empty and leaving filled but was unable to find out where they were going.

Not knowing what was happening was obviously most disturbing to Mama and Aunt Nanny. There was little that could be done since none of the Jewish agencies that had previously served the Jewish community seemed to be in operation. One fact became apparent, however, based on our personal observations and later supplemented by reports from friends and acquaintances; any Jew, especially any male Jew, walking on the streets, if recognized by roaming gangs of S.A. thugs, was beaten or severely abused. Roaming gangs of four to six S.A. men in full uniform and carrying sticks or truncheons were seen on almost every street. That afternoon Inge and I, stimulated by the day's activities, could not tear ourselves away from the window to watch the goings on. Within a short time we saw several of these gangs roaming back and forth on our street.

While watching the activities on this busy thoroughfare, we saw one of the gangs chasing a fast running Jung man wearing an overcoat that was open and flying in the breeze. Soon they all were out of viewing range, but there was no doubt that this was one of the hundreds of anti-Semitic episodes of the day. My thoughts at the moment were: Good, they can't catch him, but I also could not understand why they were doing this to him, to us Jews. What had we done? What had uncle Sigmund done that he was taken by the police? What is wrong with us that we are being persecuted? My mind was full of questions, the answers to which I could not fathom. This was the day after the burning and destruction and the roundup of the Jewish men. At that time the yellow star of identification was not yet required on clothing; the only way to identify Jews on the street was by their looks or actions or by confronting them. Our family members did not have conspicuously Jewish appearances, so we could meld into a crowd or walk the streets in relative anonymity, but Inge and I were scared, and as instructed by Mama we did not go on the street that day. The most sensible thing to do was to stay off the streets, but since Mama had to go out, whenever she saw S.A. men, she slipped into the nearest apartment house lobby or side street. On the following days we found out that several men we knew, who had escaped the roundup of Jewish men, including Franz Hamburger and our English tutor, had been attacked on the street and were severely beaten by S.A. gangs. A number of Jewish women and children were likewise attacked. This kind of random violence had previously not been common in Frankfurt, but most startling was the realization that the police did not intervene.

In the absence of accurate information about the fate of the arrested Jewish men, rumors multiplied and spread with amazing rapidity. Some of the rumors: the men were taken away to be shot, the men were being taken to concentration camps, the men were being shipped to other cities to repair the damaged Jewish property, the men were being put in jail, the men were taken to farms to help with the harvest. All we really knew was that almost all Jewish adult men of Frankfurt, over ten thousand of them, had been taken into custody, amassed at the Messehalle, and none of us knew where they were taken. Also, anyone could see with his own eyes the destruction of practically every Jewish-owned store and almost all synagogues. Out of almost one hundred synagogues in Frankfurt, only one large and a few small synagogues remained. All the others were completely destroyed or so damaged that they were immediately torn down to the ground. Jewish stores would no longer be allowed to operate.

On the evening of November 10, news broadcasts announced that the German people had "spontaneously" retaliated against the Jewish murder of Ernst von Rath. Furthermore, the Jews would be required to pay a fine of one billion *Reichsmarks* (250 million dollars) for his death plus 250 million Reichsmarks to repair the streets, lampposts, and other property damaged during the uprising of the German Volk.

After two days of hell, the orgy of anti-Jewish disorders abated. About a week later, Uncle Sigmund returned. Together with other Jewish men from the Frankfurt area, he had been transported to the Buchenwald Concentration Camp. At an *Appell* (assembly) in front of their barracks, several days after arrival, they were asked if any of them had been members of the German armed forces in World War I, and had received any awards for bravery or wounds. Uncle Sigmund, fortunately, had been awarded the Iron Cross first-class. This was attested to in his identification paper (*Ausweis*). Every teenage and adult German was required to carry an Ausweis at all times and so Uncle Sigmund was able to show his. Having shown proof of his military award of more than twenty years before, he was allowed to return home.

When he returned, he had lost some weight, but more obvious he had lost parts of his front teeth. He was a changed man, who focused on leaving Germany as quickly as possible.

Before November 9, he had always said that he would be able to survive the Nazi regime by living conservatively and inconspicuously in Frankfurt where he was relatively unknown and blended in. He was now fully convinced of the need to leave Germany immediately.

Telegrams to and from Uncle Salli in England resulted in permission for the Stahl family—Sigmund, Nanny, and Ilse—to get a visitor permit to England. I was never privy to the details, but I still recall accompanying them to the Frankfurt airport where they waved to us as they boarded the plane. This was the first time I had been to an airport and the first time I saw an airplane close at hand. I thought it was all very glamorous. They soon were airborne, and although their papers indicated "temporary visit," they had no intention of returning.

Chapter 8

My Last Months in Germany

After November 10, the attacks by S.A. men gradually diminished, but no tranquility was left. It was gone! Since we had no telephone, we communicated with relatives by word of mouth and by letters. Mother also tried to talk to others, particularly non-Jews, to gage the national sentiment. After the events of November ninth and tenth, there were no Jews left in Germany who were not convinced that there were absolutely no prospects of making a living in that country as long as Hitler was in power. This opinion was not universal before, but now it was reinforced by any conversation on this subject with non Jews that would still talk to Jews. This sentiment was further confirmed by the "official" news. National news was gleaned from the illegal radios many Jewish families kept despite the law making it illegal for Jews to own a radio, and from newspapers. We did not have a radio because Mother felt that having one was not worth the risk of arrest. We occasionally bought a newspaper, realizing that all content therein was government approved, and hence very biased. The news never seemed to be good from our point of view.

The week after Kristall Nacht, school resumed, but now the pressure to leave Germany was visible to me in school. Every few days another student or teacher was gone, reported to have emigrated. Before long classes were combined and occasionally canceled. It was clear that the once highly rated school was in it's last spasms of educational life.

A new national ordinance was issued that all Jews must incorporate a "Jewish" name into their given name. The name "Israel" must be added to male names. For females, the additional name of "Sarah" must be used. Thus, my name became Werner Israel Neubürger. Only people with very "Jewish" names like Isaac, Moses, Abraham or Rebecca did not need to adopt this additional name. Also, everyone's Ausweis (identification paper) was to be stamped with a large red "J" to identify the carrier as a Jew. When identifying yourself at any government facility it was required to humble and humiliate yourself in that you state that you are a Jew and then state your new Jewish name ("I am the Jew Werner Israel Neuburger").

Mother, who was desperately trying to figure out a way to get us out of Germany, saw the name requirement as an opportunity. She managed to have my father's quota application amended with the letter "I" for Israel. Then, using what I later found out to be bribery, she managed to have my father's application amended again so that the "I" was spelled out as Ingeborg, my sister's name. Now my father's quota application included Louis and Ingeborg. Next she applied for a change on the application from Louis to Helen since Louis had died, and Ingeborg was a minor. It took papers and money and much finagling, but she finally succeeded. Now the remaining problem was twofold. The quota number was expected to be called by late 1939 or early 1940; she'd have to budget tightly to manage until then. But worse than that, I was not on the quota application, and all her efforts to get me on failed. What to do now?

Mother investigated possibilities by means of the remaining Jewish aid organizations. One seemed to meet our needs. "The Inter-Aid Committee for Children, a British-Jewish aid society, was working with the Frankfurt Jewish organization The Center of Jewish Children's Affairs. They were organizing children's transports (Kinder transports) to England. This program consisted of sending German Jewish children, most from 10 to 13 years old, to England where British families agreed to care for them and possibly to adopt them. Officially, the English government was willing to accept these children for educational purposes, but in reality the effort was to get Jewish children out of Germany since there was no future for them in Germany, and it was only a matter of time before the entire Jewish educational system in Germany would collapse for lack of funds and teachers. By this time absolutely no Jewish children in Germany were permitted to attend non-Jewish schools. The Jewish schools suffered from the loss of financial supporters, the exodus of teachers and students, and frequent interference by the Nazis. Such interference manifested itself by government orders forbidding the use of certain textbooks, ordering the removal of specific books from the school libraries, and monitoring random class sessions by Nazi officials. My homeroom teacher, Doctor Bick was a very proud man and often commented negatively on these hindrances to our education.

I met the qualifications for Kinder transport and soon thereafter was scheduled to be on a trainload of children, mostly boys, scheduled to leave Frankfurt for England in July 1939. I still had several months in Germany prior to my departure. Mama hoped that once in England I would eventually be able to get to America, possibly with Uncle Salli's help. Her efforts to get cousin Gerd on a Kinder transport failed because he was too young.

Life for me now was a waiting game. Go to school, stay out of trouble, and keep a low profile. This was a difficult time for me, not only because of the way I had to live, but because I feared the unknown. The thought of leaving Mama and Inge made me shiver whenever I thought of being away from them and going to a strange new place. These thoughts were on my mind quite often, especially at night as I tried to go to sleep.

Mother was a stately and attractive 39-year-old woman, more than five feet, six inches tall. Her outlook always was as positive as possible, but I did not fully realize her bravery and courage until one incident in late 1938. Late in the afternoon someone knocked at our front door. Mama opened the door. There stood an S.A. man in full uniform, slightly built, but quite imposing. Like a typical S.A. man, he wore hobnailed boots with the lower legs sheathed in leather puttees. A wide leather belt and diagonal shoulder strap held up brown breeches. The brown shirt featured a red armband with a white circle and black swastika. A brown tie was flanked by swastika pins on the shirt collar. To enhance his stature he wore a stiff-sided cap adorned with a swastika. The cap had a dark leather visor and a similarly dark leather chin-strap. He said he had orders to search our apartment for contraband. When Mother asked to see his order, he retorted that he didn't have to show his papers to a Jewess. Mother remained firmly in a position blocking the door as he stood in the hallway outside. He apparently studied her with a bit of a leer on his face and then suggested that with her cooperation he could make the operation quite pleasant. Mother must have sensed by his change of tone that his authorization was questionable and his intentions even more so. A rush of adrenaline must have surged through her body. She grabbed him by the top of the tie and pushed him back so that she could slam the door on him. In that moment of defensive action, she shouted that she would inform the police supervisor if he made any further attempts at illegal entry. The police officer she named was the only police officer's name that came to her mind. It was the official she had talked to regarding Sigmund on November 10. Inge and I cowered in the background, barely out of sight but witnessing the whole episode. With the door slammed shut and locked, we retreated to the end of our hallway and embraced each other in nervous exhaustion. Nothing further happened with this thug.

One day in early 1939, we received a package from Uncle Salli containing sugar, coffee, rice, and corn flakes. We recognized the first three as precious commodities but could not decipher how to use the corn flakes. We had never seen such an item and did not know enough English to figure out any instructions there may have been on how to prepare this food for eating. Making a guess, Mama decided to serve it in a bowl with hot water poured over it. It was a mushy but interesting meal.

It was our good fortune that the apartment we lived in was not in a Jewish neighborhood and faced the main street, Mainzer Landstrasse, which always bore traffic. We thus did not have the frequent vandalism directed against Jews that other parts of Frankfurt, especially the eastern part experienced during the spring of 1939.

Mother, Inge and I prior to my going to England, 1939.

Chapter 9

Kinder Transport

Eventually, the time came for my Kinder transport. Mama made sure that all arrangements were taken care of, and on July 6, 1939, Inge and Mama accompanied me to the *Hauptbahnhof* (main railroad station) where they hugged me and gave me farewell kisses that would have to last a long time. I had very mixed feelings. On the one hand, I was scared at the thought of leaving the two people with whom I had spent my entire life. On the other hand, I was stimulated by all the attention and the prospect of an adventurous trip. Mama assured me that Uncle Salli would be there if I needed him. I started to shiver, my reaction to nervous tension, but tried to pull myself together and boarded the train, together with about 300 other children and a few chaperones. Our luggage was limited to what each of us could carry. I had two suitcases. One contained my clothing. The other was packed with an assortment of things including a sandwich, a portable chess game given to me by a friend as a farewell present, my stamp collection, and some small gifts. I also had 10 Deutschmarks (the equivalent of about two dollars and fifty cents) in my pocket and around my neck a large tag with my identification number, which each child on the transport received and which we were requested to keep around our neck. Although I vaguely knew several fellow travelers from school, I felt sorely lonely as soon as the train left the station. I had been on a train only twice before, once when my father took me to the eye doctor in Marburg and once when we moved to Frankfurt. Traveling by train was still a new and exciting experience for me.

After several hours that seemed like an eternity, we arrived at the Dutch border. The train stopped. Officials went through our car, counting heads and checking papers carried by our chaperone and checking our tag numbers against their lists. The mood was tense and my fear was that if I were to be ordered off the train, what would I do? To my and everyone's relief the dour officials left. The train started again and moved a short distance, across the border. Then it stopped again on the Dutch side. Here, women came to the windows with cups of hot chocolate. They looked friendly and tried to communicate with us, but I could not understand them. The gesture of hot chocolate spoke for itself, and soon we partook of second and third helpings and expressed our appreciation by saying *"Danke schön"* (Thank you very much). They seemed to understand and nodded and smiled. How wonderful—and they did not charge any money.

Soon, the train began moving again through the flat but scenic Dutch countryside. It was getting dark when we arrived at Zeebrugge. Here, we left the train and boarded a ship for the cross-Channel ride to Harwich, England. I must have slept for most of this channel crossing because I seem to remember being awakened by another child with whom I soon shared the excitement of landfall and docking. We debarked early in the morning at Harwich and proceeded through immigration. I received an identification document that contained my personal particulars, a picture of me, and an official seal. This document, which I still have, stated on it's backside: "Leave to land granted at Harwich this day (7 July 1939) on condition that the holder does not enter any employment paid or unpaid while in the United Kingdom." After exiting the immigration area, we were given white bread sandwiches and lemonade. I recall this since it seemed like a strange breakfast, especially the white bread. I never had such white mushy bread.

Next we boarded a train to London. Again, our train car was filled exclusively with Kinder transport children. It was on this train ride that I acquired two new words of English; "vacant" and "occupied." It seemed that everyone had drunk too much lemonade for breakfast and was now in need of the one toilet in the car.

After perhaps an hour or two, we arrived at a railroad station in London. From there we were led to a large hall and seated, like an audience, in front of an elevated stage occupied by a number of women at a large table. Next to us were several rows of seats occupied by adults. We were, of course, very apprehensive. Everything seemed strange and different. In Germany, even in the cosmopolitan city of Frankfurt, I did not remember seeing women as elegantly attired and sophisticated as these were, except on holidays. I could not recall having seen women smoking or wearing lipstick. These women had brightly colored lips and unnaturally red cheeks. They were exceptionally well groomed and attractive. It did not take long for the rumor to spread that they were actresses.

In reality they were volunteer ladies from the Inter Aid Committee who were now in process of matching the children with the English families who had volunteered to accept them.

I focused my attention on the part of the hall where the adopters were seated, in the hope of recognizing a stranger I had never seen or even heard of. Which of them would be my future guardian? Scanning the adults, to my wonderful surprise, I spotted my Uncle Salli, talking to a man next to him. That man seemed about the same age and physical type as my uncle. Could it be that I was going to Uncle Salli? What exquisite good fortune that would be!

After a wait that seemed eternal but was really not a very long time, my name was called together with the number on my identification tag. I rushed forward and was warmly greeted by Uncle Salli. He quickly explained that the two-bedroom flat he was living in was already jammed to the hilt by Sigmund, Nanny, Ilse, and himself. However, he had arranged for his friends, the Lasnick family, to volunteer to take care of me. He then introduced me to Doctor Abe Lasnick, who gave me a big friendly smile, a gentlemanly hug, and led me to one of the volunteer ladies to complete the paperwork so that we could be off to his home.

The three of us left and walked to the nearby parking spot. Dr. Lasnick drove as Uncle Salli and I sat in the back seat. Uncle Salli was anxious to hear all about the family and the recent events in Germany. I spoke in German, and he translated my conversation into English since Abe Lasnick did not know German.

When we arrived at the Lasnick home at 13 Cleveland Road in Ealing, just west of London, I was greeted by the whole Lasnick family. There were Mr. and Mrs. Lasnick, who were probably in their late 50s or early 60s. They had three unmarried grown children, Abe, the oldest, now a doctor, Ray and Mary, two daughters in their late twenties or early thirties—and a wonderful and typically stubborn British bulldog named "Boy." They desperately tried to convey a warm welcome to me. Although I did not understand what they were saying, I could sense their good intentions.

They lived in a comfortable two-story free-standing house with a fully enclosed back yard, and a small walk-in greenhouse attached to one side of the house. Downstairs there was a combination kitchen and family room, a walk-in pantry, and a formal living/dining room as well as a hallway and staircase to the upstairs, where there were four bedrooms and a bathroom.

Ray, the middle sibling, took charge. She and Salli showed me my room, a small but pleasant bedroom all for myself. Yes,

Ray is the female and Salli is the male. Then Uncle Salli explained that he had to go back to his dental office since he had patients scheduled and waiting. He told me he would see me on the weekend when he would pick me up to take me to his house for the day. There Uncle Sigmund, Aunt Nanny, and Ilse were anxiously waiting to greet me. Before leaving, he reached into his pocket, pulled out some coins and introduced me to British currency by showing me a crown (ten shilling), a half crown, a shilling, six pence, a penny, a half penny and a farthing. He explained their relationship and the approximate German mark equivalents and then left them all for me to keep. As he left, I suddenly felt deserted, but when I noticed him giving Ray a kiss on the cheek, I felt just a little relieved.

Ray helped me unpack, showed me the house and garden, and let me hold Boy's leash when it was time to take him for a walk. We walked about two blocks to a park-like area, which she tried to explain was the English common. Language was a really big problem. I could not understand any words she said, and she was unable to understand me. I had learned some English, but whenever I wanted to say something, I could not find the right words. Undoubtedly, this strange new environment exacerbated my already strained nerves. The language problem was especially acute on the first evening when the whole family sat around the formal dining table to welcome me with a really good meal. By that time I was extremely hungry but ate only the food put on my plate as politely as I could. I would have loved to have had second helpings, especially another slice of bread, but I did not understand their offer (if they made any). I was too bashful to ask for more in German, and I just did not know how to ask in English. That first night I went to bed feeling hungry, lonely, and homesick. I recall I cried myself to sleep.

Chapter 10

England

Although I acquired some rudimentary English fairly quickly, at the time it seemed as if it took forever. Frustration and lack of self-esteem were my dominant feelings. To assist in my learning English and to avoid interrupting my education, the Lasnicks enrolled me in a private all-boys school, Harrow View House, located on Cleveland Road, just a few houses away from where I lived. It was a small school, formerly an estate house consisting of perhaps twenty rooms, of which about twelve were classrooms. The school was unique for me in that it was a middle school having only three grades, the equivalent of sixth, seventh and eighth grade. Classes were small with about ten to twelve students in each class. The entire student population was not much larger than one hundred.

During classes the teachers, all male, wore black academic gowns over their suits. They were at all times addressed as "sir." We students all wore dark blue jackets, matching short pants, "Eaton" caps, knee socks, and white shirt with tie. The jacket breast pocket had the school logo emblazoned on it. Wearing the school uniform gave me a sense of equality, which made me feel quite good, as though I was part of the system. The curriculum, however, was way over my head. Two foreign languages were compulsory: Latin or Greek, and German or French. Latin and German were selected for me. English, geography, mathematics, science, history, literature, and athletics were my other subjects. Most of the teachers spoke reasonably good German and tried to help me, but my frustration manifested itself in every subject.

I had never been exposed to Latin, so that was a complete loss. Even German was a tour in frustration. The teacher would say or write something in German, and I would understand it but would not know the English equivalent and thus could not supply the requested translation. If he said or wrote something in English to be translated into German, I would not know the meaning of the words in English.

Geography and mathematics were the two subjects in which I had limited success, but even here my lack of English and especially its pronunciation created stress and frustration. I recall a geography lesson in which a map of Europe was displayed, the teacher pointed to a city, and then asked a student to identify it. I believe he tried to favor me by selecting cities I knew. When he pointed to Frankfurt, I quickly raised my hand. He queried; "Master Neuburger (we were always addressed this way), what city is that?" I proudly answered "Frankfurt am Main" in my best German pronunciation. My fellow students snickered at my apparent mispronunciation of the *a* in Frankfurt. My *a* was pronounced like the *a* in arm and not like the *a* in can.

My two greatest handicaps were first, the language, and second the unfortunate circumstance that I was enrolled in the school in June, well into the semester. In August the school year would end, scheduled to reconvene in September. As part of the end-of-semester activities, there was an athletic event, an outing, at the commons. Since I did not know the rules of the games such as football (soccer), cricket, or relay racing, I was excused from participating in those activities. In an effort to have me partake in something, I was told to participate in an obstacle race. However, even here, when instructions were given, I did not understand them. I followed as well as I could and came in last. I felt like crying and running away, but I knew this was the last day at school, so I went to the refreshment stand and tried to make myself inconspicuous and stuffed myself with cookies and lemonade.

When Ray came to pick me up at the end of activities, she asked whether I had had a good time. I said, "*Nein*," and then corrected myself and said, "No, not really." Although my answer was negative, she was so pleased with my converting to English that she gave me a warm hug. It made me feel a lot better.

Every evening the entire family would gather around the radio in the living room to listen to news broadcasts. I tried but just could not understand what the newscasters were saying. I caught a few words but not the meaning. Ray and Mary tried to explain that Hitler had been and was continuing to do bad things. He was repeatedly violating the peace treaty that Germany had signed at the end of World War I. Until that time I had not realized that Germany was misbehaving with respect to the outside world. I had assumed that the only bad things the Germans were doing were against the Jews of Germany, and even those actions were beyond my comprehension. I could not grasp why the demagogic efforts of the Nazis were directed against the Jews as the enemy. Since Germany had always been my home, I had an inborn affinity for it. After all, my family had lived there for generations. I do remember that I was thoroughly confused and experienced a strong feeling of insecurity and loneliness. If I could only be with my mother!

I knew that this treaty (the Versailles Treaty signed at the Palace of Versailles in France after Germany lost the war of 1914–1918) put limits on German rearmament. The treaty stated that Germany could have an army of only 100,000 men.

Germany could not have an air force and was only supposed to have a limited navy. According to the treaty, it was not allowed to station any troops west of the Rhine River, thus creating a non-military buffer zone between France and Germany. The treaty also established Austria, Poland and Czechoslovakia as independent countries. There were many other aspects to this treaty, but these were the most troublesome ones from the German perspective. To a large extent, while in Germany, I had absorbed the German propaganda that these treaty requirements were unfair, but as a twelve-year-old these were not of serious consequence to me. I was more concerned by the daily events that affected my life more directly.

Hitler had first violated the treaty by enlarging his army beyond the allowed maximum He then created a modern air force and enlarged his navy. In 1936, German troops had marched into the Rheinland. In 1938, Germany annexed the entire country of Austria. Cowering before Hitler's bullying, the other European countries, especially England and France, did nothing about these treaty violations. Next Hitler claimed that Germans living in Czechoslovakia were being mistreated and that part of Czechoslovakia must go to Germany. Responding to the threat of aggression, the French and English prime ministers met with Hitler in Munich, Germany. They agreed to let him take the part of Czechoslovakia, which had many residents of German descent, a region known as the Sudetenland. This was offered on the condition that there would be no further territorial requests by Hitler. Hitler agreed to this condition. When English Prime Minister Neville Chamberlain returned to England after this meeting in Munich in the fall of 1938, he pronounced the now infamous message: "I have obtained peace in our time!" How wrong he was. I had hardly remembered that episode, but during the summer of 1939, Ray refreshed my memory of that event and tried to convey to me that in the fall of 1938, many thought that the Prime Minister had saved the world from war. That peace now seemed to be in jeopardy. War to me at that time did not mean the same as it does today. My image of war then was heroic combat and adventure rather than destruction and death. What did twelve-year-old boys know about war in 1939?

In March 1939, Hitler's army occupied the rest of Czechoslovakia. The extinction of what was left of Czechoslovakia also extinguished England and France's policy of appeasement. Chamberlain announced that if Hitler were to target any other country, England and France would come to that country's aid and war would ensue. Meanwhile, Hitler's propaganda machine created horror stories about atrocities being committed upon Germans living in Poland. This was the current state of affairs as we listened to the evening radio broadcasts. Ray tried hard to explain the daily news to me, supplementing such news with relevant past events. My confusion needed clearing up, and furthermore, I expressed a sincere interest in learning what was happening and why. With Ray's and Mary's concentrated efforts, my comprehension of world events as well as my understanding of English improved rapidly. Soon, I could speak the language well enough for basic conversation, and I had acquired an understanding of Hitler's unrelenting march to war. Since much of my family, especially Mama and Inge, were still in Germany, my concerns, rather than being alleviated, were constantly grinding in my mind. I wished I were not away from them.

Uncle Salli and Ray occasionally took me along to the movies or to Uncle Salli's home. Other than walks to the commons and playing occasional games such as chess, checkers and Monopoly there was little entertainment for me. I did not read books because my English was still too limited. In late summer of 1939, Uncle Salli, who frequently had visited us, paying special attention to Ray, stopped visiting. I soon found out that Ray had been under the impression that Salli intended to marry her. He apparently did not have that intention, so they decided not to continue their relationship. Under these circumstances,

Uncle Salli suggested that I come to live with him and the Stahls, but the Lasnicks insisted that I stay with them. I had become very much part of their family. Before long all agreed that I should stay with the Lasnicks. I did, however, visit Salli, Sigmund, Nanny and Ilse every few weeks by myself, using the Underground transit. Fortunately, the line starting in Ealing went almost directly to Whitechapple, East London, where Salli had his home on Commercial Road. I had to change trains only once at Liverpool Street Station. The Underground stop at Whitechapple was right at the start of Commercial Road. Then I could walk to Number 330, Uncle Salli's house.

He lived in a house attached to similar houses on both sides. It had three floors, with two rooms and stairwell/hallway on each floor. On the first floor was a waiting room and the office where he practiced dentistry. The second floor had a kitchen and a living room, which also served as Ilse's bedroom. The third floor had two bedrooms, one for Uncle Salli and one for Sigmund and Nanny. The toilet was in an outhouse in the back yard. Yes, I was surprised that here in the middle of London the toilet was outside the house. All the rooms were rather small and heated only by fireplaces. In the winter, it was difficult to be comfortable. The side of you facing the fireplace was overheated and the other side of you was cold. Fireplace wood was expensive, so it was sparingly used. I was always very welcome at my uncle's home. Nanny was kept busy taking care of the house and cooking, but I could sense the frustration of Ilse and Sigmund, who were relatively idle helping Nanny, but in reality without meaningful work. It was a condition of their visitors permit that they could not engage in any paying jobs. Furthermore they could not get working permits, and most significantly, there was the danger of being expelled from the country if they were caught violating this ordinance. England had serious unemployment and did not want foreigners to aggravate this condition. Uncle Salli barely made enough money to support the family. The effects of the lingering depression and unemployment were very evident in England in 1939.

The school year ended, and the summer vacation started. Kenneth, a young cousin of Ray and Mary, came to visit us. Kenneth was a year older than I was and was great company. He visited frequently and taught me much about the English way of looking at things. Words like *equality* and *democracy* were alien to me in Germany. I had only overheard these words in adult conversation when they were used in derogatory form. Especially the word *democracy* was used in conversation as denoting decadence and lack of respect. That was the image I had of these words before Kenneth gave me a new explanation. Kenneth and I developed a very close friendship. He was not a stamp collector, but when I showed him my collection of mostly German stamps, he was aghast that most of them had Hitler's countenance on them. He could not understand how I could possibly want them. I had to agree with him, so we took the stamps that had Hitler's image or a swastika on them and with gusto tore them into pieces. Thus, I lost the bulk of my stamp collection for the second time.

One morning when Kenneth and I were walking Boy through the commons, a strange sound pierced the air. It was the sound of sirens, not just one, but many sounds coming from all different directions. Kenneth thought they were air raid sirens, and we rushed home. Yes, indeed they were air raid sirens. England had just declared war on Germany. Germany had invaded Poland on September 1, and Hitler refused the ultimatum to withdraw. Consequently, both England and France declared war. This was the day on which I heard the sirens for the first time, September 3, 1939, the beginning of World War II.

I turned thirteen the following week. Uncle Salli asked me to come to his home early on the following Saturday. He and Uncle Sigmund took me to a small synagogue nearby where I was, for the first time in my life, given a *tallis* (prayer shawl) and called up to be a witness to the reading of the Torah and to say the respective blessings. This was my Bar Mitzvah. After services we went back to Salli's house where Aunt Nanny had prepared a delicious meal. Throughout that day I very much missed my mother and sister. How I wished that I could have shared this occasion with them! Late that afternoon I went back to the Lasnick's house. When I went to bed that night, I looked out the window from my bed and saw the moon, large and clear. *Mother and Inge are seeing this same moon*, I thought, and felt that perhaps we were not that far away from each other after all.

The sirens Kenneth and I heard on September 3 had been activated as a test and to alert the British people that a state of war existed. Several days thereafter, subsequent to the destruction of its cities, Poland succumbed to the German blitzkrieg of heavy armor and dive bombers, and Russia's invasion of Poland from the east.

For the next few weeks, we heard the sirens several times as unidentified or German aircraft were spotted nearby. Apparently Germany had, at various times, sent probing flights and reconnaissance planes over France and England. In view of the potential danger of bombings, most children in London, especially in affluent areas, were evacuated to the country. The Lasnicks decided to keep me with them, but they did contract to have an air raid shelter built in their back yard.

Air raid shelters became a common backyard addition and were of fairly standard design. Made of corrugated steel with a curved roof, they were about 12 feet long, 10 feet wide and 7 feet high in the middle, where the two curved sides met. Each side had a bench that could be used as a cot with storage underneath. Stored items included preserved food, water and first aid kit, and blankets. A kerosene lantern and a small stove were kept in the back. In the rear corner, behind a curtain, was a potty. The shelters were almost half below ground level. Inside the door, or rather a hatch, several steps led down into the shelter. In the spring of 1940, after several bombs were dropped in our area, we were told to go in it whenever there was an air raid. However, we only did so when we actually heard nearby anti-aircraft guns firing.

Gas masks were issued to everyone. Carrying gas masks at all times outside the home became mandatory. The gas masks initially came in square cardboard boxes with shoulder strings, but soon commercial entrepreneurs offered fancier cloth containers in a multiplicity of designs. Air raid wardens were a common sight. The war created an additional vocabulary for me with terms such as blackout, shelter, air raid, barrage balloon, anti aircraft. The war also meant the end of my correspondence with my mother. This was a big blow to me.

With most of the students evacuated, Harrow View House did not reopen for classes. After hearing that I would remain in the neighborhood, the headmaster came to visit us in late September and wondered if I might help keep the grounds in order since the groundskeeper had gone into the army. The Lasnicks considered this as an honor and said I would, and I acquiesced. The grounds consisted of perhaps an acre of landscaped flower beds, bushes, many trees, a pattern of serpentine walks and some lawn. The area was enclosed by an iron fence faced with hedges. So now almost every morning I spent some time weeding, mowing, and keeping the grounds tidy. Of course, the mower was a non-motorized push mower. Mary helped me occasionally, and Kenneth did too when he came to visit. Occasionally the headmaster would stop by and give me some pointers and a compliment. His periodic visits did keep me aware that I had committed to an obligation. I certainly did not want to disappoint him, and I hoped this service might help me in the forthcoming school year. My thoughts were that if I did a good job, at least he should not flunk me. Besides, I enjoyed gardening. It reminded me a little of my life in Battenberg.

Since I could no longer communicate with Mother in Germany, I started to write to my relatives in the United States, the Eliases, Lowensterns[6], and Simons. Not that I wrote often, but perhaps one letter per month, generally in response to letters from them. They could still write and receive letters from Germany and so kept me a little bit informed of news from there. Such tidbits of information is what motivated me to write. I read that Mama and Inge were in good health but that food was becoming more and more scarce (especially for Jews), that Inge could no longer attend school, that emigration (to the United States) was their sole hope, that the Eliases were trying everything possible to get Mama and Inge out of Germany and hoped to succeed soon.

In early 1940, the British government changed leadership, and Winston Churchill became Prime Minister. England noticeably changed to a full war footing. I watched Home Guard soldiers drilling in the commons. They were mostly men who were too old to join the regular army. There were frequent air raids in which bombs were dropped, but never near us. "The Blitz," in which so much of London was destroyed, did not start until late spring of 1940. At this time, however, there was still evidence of war. Military trucks became a common sight. Barrage balloons by the thousands were all over the London sky. They were shaped like miniature Zeppelins and were tethered with cables, with many extra cables dangling from their periphery. These extra cables were intended to entangle German dive bombers and keep German aircraft above a certain altitude so as to diminish their bombing accuracy. The balloons floated at various altitudes. Also, wrecked automobiles were placed in the commons and other parks to prevent German gliders from landing in the open meadows.

So far there was little activity on the German front. At this time of the war, the British and French were protected by the

---

[6] As they arrived in the United States, most family names that contained an umlaut dropped that umlaut from their name spelling.

England, 1939
Left to right: Ray Lasnick, Uncle Sigmund,
Mary and Mrs. Lasnick, Aunt Nanny.

"Maginot Line," a continuous series of heavily fortified facilities all along the French border with Germany. The Germans were dug in along a similar defensive line called "The Siegfried Line." Neither side seemed ready to do any serious fighting at this time, just minor skirmishing.

In March 1940 I received a letter from Aunt Else Elias saying that Mama and Inge were on their way from Germany to America and that the necessary paperwork was under way to get me to America soon. Since there was less emigration from Germany now, it was not too difficult to get a visa under the German quota (for German refugees) from England to the United States.

Uncle Salli confirmed the story. My world had suddenly changed again. I would be going to America with the Stahls. When the headmaster of Harrow View House heard that I was to leave soon, he again came to visit to thank me for my work and gave me a crisp 10 shilling note (the equivalent of about two dollars). I considered this extremely generous and so expressed myself.

The Lasnick family were woefully sad to have me leave but happy that I could rejoin my family. Abe Lasnick gave me a note that I still have.

> *Werner Neuburger (age 13) has been staying with me since his arrival from Germany about eight months ago. He has been a good boy, honest, obedient and willing to please.*
>
> *A, Lasnick MBBS, CRCP, MRCS.*

Uncle Salli purchased my ship passage ticket and a new suitcase. On April 6, 1940, the three members of the Stahl family and I embarked from Liverpool on the S.S. *Scythia*.

Chapter 11

America

Because of frequent sinkings of British ships by the German U boats, the S.S. *Scythia* moved at close to top speed through stormy seas and rainy weather in a zigzag course. Altogether, this caused almost every passenger aboard to become seasick. The Stahls and I shared one cabin with four beds, two uppers and two lowers. I was seasick most of the time on the passage to America, where we arrived on the 19th of April, 1940.

While the ocean crossing was relatively uneventful, the opposite was true for the war in Europe. A news bulletin was issued on the ship each day. Three days into the trip, on April 9, 1940, we read the astonishing news that Hitler's military juggernaut had invaded Denmark and Norway. My recollection of the consensus of the passengers was that now Hitler had chewed off more than he could digest. The next day however, we read with dismay that Denmark had surrendered without a fight. The consensus now was disappointment. Thereafter, the daily bulletins were filled with tidbits of news relating to Norwegian resistance and Britain's aid in the form of troops and naval forces. The British and Norwegian efforts, however, were unable to offer much resistance. By the time we reached the United States, the fighting was still going on, but the outlook was reported as grim. We were disappointed that the Germans were successful but hoped against hope that the tables might still turn. They did not turn. Although I did not fully realize it then, this action by Hitler sent threatening signals to the other countries of Europe. There could be no legal justification for the invasion of these nations, and this unprovoked offensive attack was a forerunner of further "might is right" aggression by Germany.

As we approached New York harbor, early in that misty morning, the Stahls and I together with most of the other passengers were on deck, each trying to be first to spot the famous symbol of America, the Statue of Liberty. Each buoy and floating marker along the harbor approach seemed to me, from a distance, to be the treasured sight. Finally Ilse, standing next to me on the crowded rail, shouted in a definitive tone, "I see it!" and there it was in majestic glory even more so than I had imagined. It certainly was much larger than the several falsely acclaimed buoys and bobbing navigation devices we saw earlier. Slowly the ship moved towards the impressive lower Manhattan skyline and indeed the skyscrapers looked like they were touching the clouds, which hung low in the sky that morning. When our ship docked at a Manhattan west side pier in New York Harbor, I was happy to have landed but apprehensive as to what would happen next. Passengers were called by name over the ship's loudspeakers as their debarkation papers were processed. My name was called before the Stahls'. Uncle Sigmund went with me to the debarkation desk where he was rudely told to wait his turn and that someone was here at the dock to meet me. How they knew that I don't know. As we looked down to the pier we saw Manfred Marx, the son of my father's cousin (Louis Marx), accompanied by my former Battenberg playmate, Hannelore Stern.

I said my goodbyes to Uncle Sigmund, Aunt Nanny, and Ilse and walked down the gangplank, lugging my heavy suitcase. It contained all my worldly possessions. At the base of the gangplank I met my reception committee of two. Manfred and his family had visited us several times back in Battenberg. Hannelore had grown into an attractive teenager, and her friendliness and cheerfulness had not changed. After warm embraces, we walked to the subway and soon arrived at the Sterns' home on 141st Street near Broadway in upper Manhattan.

My first impression of New York was that it was noisy, dirty, busy, and not as glamorous as I had anticipated. From the ship to 141st Street, I saw no skyscrapers and none of the elegantly dressed people as I had anticipated, but what did impress me was the extensive display of fruits and vegetables in the several green markets extending onto the sidewalk as we walked from the subway station to the Sterns' apartment. The apartment was not large, but I was impressed by modern conveniences such as a refrigerator and a toilet with soft perforated toilet paper, hot and cold running water, and a bathtub with shower in the bathroom.

The Sterns' ebullient greetings and sincere welcome quickly made me feel at home. Apparently, my mother and the Eliases had been in contact with them, and they had enthusiastically agreed to meet me at the pier and assist me the next day in getting on the train to Utica in upstate New York. There, Mother and the Eliases would meet me.

That first evening in New York City, I felt that I was back with "my own kind." We talked at length about our experiences since parting company in Battenberg around three years previously. Those years seemed like a lifetime, and yet we immediately reestablished the common bonds that tied us together in Battenberg.

That first afternoon, Hannelore had to do a few errands and asked whether I would like to come along. Of course! We walked down several flights of stairs into a lobby, and from there onto the street. 141st Street then was a white neighborhood populated by a large number of emigrant Jews from Germany. As we walked the short distance from the front door of the apartment house to the intersection of 141st Street and Broadway, Hannelore greeted several acquaintances. How different this informality was compared to the more private lifestyle I had experienced in England. In my nine months in England, I never met any of the Lasnick's neighbors and indeed never said "hello" to anyone I passed on the street.

At the intersection we turned onto Broadway. I had envisioned Broadway as a glamorous avenue of skyscrapers and theaters, of neon lights and Hollywood. In actuality the Broadway I saw had a series of four- and five-story apartment houses with small stores on the ground floor. The fruit and vegetable stores indelibly impressed me by their extravagant displays of fruits such as bananas, pineapples, figs, cantaloupes and other fruits and vegetables that I seldom saw in Europe, especially at that time of the year. Not only was I impressed by the assortment and the large variety but also by the copious quantities. When we went into a Chinese laundry to get some of Mr. Stern's shirts, I came close to disbelief. The proprietor, a Chinese man, could barely speak English. A store-owner on Broadway who could hardly speak English and used an abacus to calculate the transaction—unbelievable!

Back at the Sterns we had a sumptuous German-style dinner like my mother used to prepare, and at this meal, unlike at my first meal in England, I could comfortably communicate my impressions and my wants. And I expressed my happiness at being back with old friends.

The next morning Manfred Marx came to pick me up and get me on the train to Utica. He told me it would take about six hours to get there and proceeded to buy me a *LIFE* magazine. I assumed it would be something like a fortuneteller's gazette. I was surprised that it was a news magazine filled with pictures about current events. As the train departed, I had a sinking feeling that Manfred had put me on the wrong train. I thought I was on a subway because the train proceeded underground for a long time. There was nothing I could do, so I just sat nervously in my seat. Finally, daylight appeared and soon the train moved alongside a huge river, the Hudson. The landscape changed from urban to rural. I was on my way to another phase of my life.

Between observing the ever-changing landscape and reading *LIFE* magazine several times, the time passed. The train reached Utica by early afternoon. As I exited, I immediately spotted my mother and Uncle Mor (short for Moritz) Elias. Mama hugged me and kissed me with tears running down her cheeks. I was equally overjoyed. My heart pounded as it never had before. We drove to the Elias home in the nearby village of New York Mills. Here, another emotional welcome awaited me from Inge, Aunt Else, and their son Mark. I did not recognize Mark as he had grown much since I last saw him more than five years ago. The others looked unchanged.

We had much news to catch up on. We were speaking in German and Uncle Mor was curious whether I could communicate in English. At his request I switched to English, only to hear him exclaim, "My, oh my, he speaks the King's English with a Battenberger accent!" Thereafter, I noticed that many Americans, especially adults, expressed some degree of fascination with my accent.

That evening a neighbor, Mr. Levit, came to greet the new arrival. When he learned about my grounds keeping experience, he said that I was just what he was looking for. Would I mow his lawn and weed the flower garden? He would of course pay me. I would get a "buck" a week. After he left, I asked, "What is a buck?" When I found out that it is one whole dollar, I quickly converted this sum in my mind to shillings and realized that in one week, I would get as much money as I had earned in England in five weeks. America seemed truly the land of golden opportunity.

It was at this time I learned about Mama's and Inge's difficult trip from Germany in February and March of 1940. Germany had an ordinance that forbade Jewish emigrants to leave with more than 10 Deutschmarks, the equivalent of about two and one-half dollars. Conversely the United States had an ordinance stating that an immigrant must posses at least 50 dollars to enter the country so that new immigrants would not become a burden to society at the time of arrival. As a substitute for $50 cash, a $500 affidavit by an American resident was acceptable. Together with the affidavit, the United States required a guarantee that the immigrant would not apply for welfare.

Faced with this conundrum, the Eliases had put up a $500 affidavit and also sent ship tickets to Inge and Mama in Germany. When their quota number came up in January 1940, they obtained their visas. Although the United States and Germany were not at war at that time, there were no direct passages from Germany to America. The tickets were for passage on an American ship, the S.S. *Washington*, sailing on February 24 from Genoa, Italy, to New York. The train trip from Frankfurt to Genoa would normally take less then a day, but to allow for any delays and to be sure to get to the ship on time they left Frankfurt on the morning of February 21.

The temptation to sneak out what little extra money she had entered my mother's mind, but she feared that in the event of a thorough search at the border, which was not at all unheard of, she might put herself and Inge in danger. The Germans were just too meticulous and especially so at checking out emigrating Jews. So she observed the law to the letter and left that God forsaken country with a total wealth of 10 Deutschmarks. She gave her remaining funds to her mother, Grandma Rosa, who remained behind with Uncle Walter and his family.

The train trip to Genoa was uneventful, and on the morning of February 22 they arrived in Genoa. There, they had to wait two days and two nights before they could board the ship, but had only 10 Deutschmarks. This would have to suffice for transportation to the pier as well as food and lodging. What to do? They did not know the Italian language, nor did they know where to turn for help. They soon discovered that in Genoa, German money was not acceptable, so they went to a bank to exchange their few Deutschmarks into Lira. The service charge reduced their funds to little more than enough to pay for two trolley rides to the pier. They decided to hold onto their few coins and spend the two days in the nearby park.

Inge took brief exploratory walks and when she observed someone eating in the park, she waited until the person finished in the hope that some of their leftovers might be thrown into the waste bin. From there she would retrieve anything that appeared edible. She was a good enough scavenger to retrieve a few morsels that kept them from getting excessively hungry.

In the meantime, Mother remained seated on the park bench, guarding the suitcases and attempting to look nonchalant. Periodically she would go for a little walk while Inge guarded the suitcases. Inge located a toilet. A nearby fountain satisfied their thirst. Fortunately, the nights, although cold, were clear and without precipitation. The Italian police noticed them but did not approach them. If the police were to questioned them, they had rehearsed their response. They would show their passports and ship tickets, and Inge would explain using a few words of Italian she had prepared before they left Germany.

It seemed like forever before the dawn of February 24 arrived. Then they boarded the trolley to the vicinity of the pier and walked to the ship berth. They boarded as early as permissible, and once aboard, their ordeal was over.

When their ship arrived in New York City, Aunt Else met them and took them to the Elias's home in New York Mills. A week later a reporter from the *Utica Observer Dispatch* visited them to get an idea what life in Germany was like. Because of their limited ability to speak English, Uncle Mor interpreted. They called America "Fairyland." They said that economic conditions in Germany were extremely serious, but even more so for them because they were Jews. With their Jewish ration cards, each was allowed an eighth of a pound of butter and one egg per week, but these allotments were further limited to three out of four weeks, and frequently the allotments were not available at all. Meat allowance was three eighths of a pound per week. No real coffee or tea was available; only coffee substitute made of malt could be obtained. Milk was limited to skimmed milk. Potatoes were available, but rice, when available, was not permitted to be sold to Jews. The newspapers no longer carried advertisements because little could be bought without authorization. Every person was allowed 100 points for clothing, but shoes were hardest of all to get. If one needed shoes very badly, she had to submit a written request and an investigator visited the home to inspect the shoes at hand. If he authorized the purchase, a pair purchased cost at least fifty marks, but the old pair had to be handed in. There were very few automobiles on the streets because of the severe shortage of gasoline, and those few were solely for official use. Most men were in the army or in Nazi uniforms of one kind or another, and thus women performed many of the jobs formerly done by men. As to the question: "How long do the Germans think the war will last?" Their response was that German people believed the "blitzkrieg" would come in the spring and that would end the war.

The interview focused on economics because of the questions put to them. Mama and Inge were at that time still so conditioned from Germany that they barely mentioned the aspects of Jewish persecution.

———•••••———

The day after I arrived in New York Mills in April 1940, Uncle Mor took Inge and me to visit the home of a friend and patient of his who was also a seventh-grade teacher in the local school,

Mrs. Finnigan. She was an experienced teacher, perhaps forty years old, quite attractive and very self confident. He asked her for guidance as to the best way to begin our American education. She suggested that Inge and I enroll in her 7th grade class at the New York Mills public school. After finishing out the school year under her guidance, she would then see to it that we were placed in the grade most appropriate for each of us.

While she reviewed the details with Uncle Mor, I tried to play with her pet dog, a Scotty. I was accustomed to playing with Boy, the Lasnick's English bulldog, but when I approached Mrs. Finnigan's Scotty he growled, and before I knew it, he jumped at me and bit my hand. I bled profusely and was in substantial pain. This episode taught me that all dogs are not of the same temperament, and it gave Mrs. Finnigan an extra touch of sympathy for me for some time thereafter. Her compassion reminded me of the teachers I had in England, but I had several advantages over my British school experience. I could now speak the language, and the curriculum was much less sophisticated: no Latin, no literature and a much less formal environment. My biggest handicap was American history, which was all new to me, but since I liked this subject, I had no compunction about reading our history textbook as though it were an adventure story. Within a few weeks I finished reading the textbook and did well on subsequent tests. Mrs. Finnigan, a strict disciplinarian, was quite generous in complimenting me, and I felt very much at ease. I did quite well on my final tests, and at the end of the school year I was transferred to the ninth grade, the first year of high school. With Mrs. Finnigan's guidance, I befriended a new classmate, Leslie Stockton. To me Leslie was the all-American boy, and he became my idol. Leslie was a third generation American. His father was a union carpenter earning the very impressive salary of $40 per week. Leslie was an outdoor person and introduced me to hiking, the Boy Scouts, model building, and American sports.

Leslie earned pocket money by delivering the *Utica Observer Dispatch*, a newspaper that almost every family in New York Mills subscribed to. I often accompanied him on his route and hinted that I was jealous of the income he earned. When Leslie heard of the availability of another newspaper route distributing the Sunday Syracuse paper and the *New York Times* Sunday edition, he helped me negotiate to get that route and a secondhand bicycle for delivering the papers. Total cost for bike and route was five dollars. It took me only a few months to recoup that sum; the Sunday papers sold for ten cents each and my take was two cents per paper. Most people left their payment each week in a prearranged location, so that I would deposit the paper and pick up the money at the same time. The acquisition of a bicycle gave me a mobility I had been longing to have.

New York Mills was a factory town with one major industry, a textile mill. This enterprise employed many of the town's men. Pay started at $16 per week and went up according to skill level. In New York Mills there was one school for all grades from one to twelve. There was one scout troop, and I felt very American when I became part of it.

On Memorial Day in 1940, our Boy Scout Troop assembled early in the morning to ride our bicycles to the nearby cemetery to place American flags on the graves of veterans of World War I, the Spanish-American War, and the Civil War. Then we marched in the parade, which featured several Civil War and Spanish-American War veterans. Some of them, in their eighties and nineties, were riding in the back of a convertible automobile.

The highest scout honor was to carry the American flag in the parade. There was some discussion as to who should carry the flag. Since I was the only new immigrant in the troop, and since the troop never before had an immigrant as a member, this great honor was given, lo and behold, to me! I could hardly hold back my tears of pride. Proudly I marched at the head of the scout troop, wearing my new wide-rimmed "campaign" hat, the flag pole resting in the leather holster with my right hand guiding the flag staff. My first American Memorial Day was an inspiring and uplifting experience. In Germany I had been excluded from all patriotic displays, but here in America I was welcomed into them. As the flag fluttered above me in the breeze, for the first time I felt that I was an American. God bless America!

When summer vacation started, one of my newspaper customers, a Mr. Hatfield, who owned a large home, asked me if I was interested in caring for his lawn and garden. Mr. Hatfield was the superintendent of the textile plant called the Knitting Mill. He offered to pay me 15 cents an hour, and he had a motorized mower to boot, a rarity in those days. I accepted gratefully and tried hard to do a good job. He recognized this and soon had me cleaning the dog kennels and helping in cleaning out the garden houses as well. Fifteen cents was substantially more than the 10 cents per hour most boys were paid for similar chores.

Shortly thereafter, several of Mr. Hatfield's neighbors asked if I'd do their lawns. Leslie and some of my other friends were looking for such work. We decided that I would take the jobs but let them do the new lawns. This worked fine for a few weeks until one of the new clients called on the telephone to complain. My uncle who answered the phone was the one to hear their complaints. They said the work was not being done properly, and they could never locate me (since I was not there). Uncle Mor then sternly insisted that I accept only work I could handle myself. He was quite disturbed and worried that his reputation would suffer. In fact, he was already in jeopardy because rumors had been circulating that he was a German spy. His pronounced German accent and his being a newcomer in an old established community may have fueled the rumors.

My entrepreneurial spirit got me into trouble on another occasion. One of the boys with whom I had become acquainted offered me a chance to earn five dollars for one day's work cleaning out cesspools. That sum was just too great to say no. My job was to climb down into the pits once the contractor's pump had emptied most of the sewage sludge. Equipped with a short shovel, I picked up the remnants and loaded them into a bucket that would be hauled up via a rope when it was full. I did my job and got paid, but when I came home reeking and stained with sewage, my aunt practically threw me out of the house. I had to try to clean myself off with the garden hose and then throw away my clothing. Not all work was worthwhile.

Another failure was my attempt at golf caddying. Leslie and his friends spent early weekend mornings in the summer serving as caddies at the exclusive Onondaga Golf Club. There, they carried golf bags for two players and generally got one dollar for each bag. In those days there were no such things as golf carts, either manual or motorized, and golfers carried their own bags or hired a caddy to carry them.

One Sunday morning, at my friend's urging, I joined Leslie and his cousin Sheldon. We rode our bikes to the clubhouse where an ante-room was designated as the place for caddies to wait to be selected. As golfers arrived, they looked over the available caddies and usually selected one who had caddied for them before. Therefore, I was passed over by every player. There were perhaps six caddies, all experienced except for me. I sat there for what seemed to me an eternity, feeling more discouraged, disheartened, and rejected as each caddy was chosen. Finally, when I was the only one left, a pair of golfers entered, asked me my name, and said, "Come on!" My spirits soared as I rose to take hold of their not-so-light golf bags.

I followed the twosome to the first tee-off green where they began their game with what appeared to me to be good swings. However, the first ball landed just short of a sand trap. When we reached the ball, the golfer studied the situation and turned to me and asked: "What do you think I should use?" I had no idea and blurted out that this was my first experience caddying and that I knew nothing about how to play and nothing about selecting clubs. Their disappointment showed clearly on their faces. As they completed the course they did not talk to me anymore. I received 50 cents from each of the two for more than four hours of heavy schlepping. This was my first and last experience as a caddy.

With my various activities I earned about $4 to $5 each week during summer vacation, but only about one and a half dollars each week while school was in session. This was considered good money, but of course I had no such thing as allowance.

In my first year of high school in New York Mills, I was anxious to learn more about the American sport of football. Leslie had shown me a little bit about the game. There was a notice in school for tryouts for the first, second and third team. I was eager to become a part of any team. At the posted time, the prospective candidates assembled on the playing field next to the school. While awaiting the coach, the fellows started to fool around, throwing the football, trying to catch it and then running a short distance before repeating that maneuver. Others tried to tackle the runner during his short sprint. Knowing my keen interest and also my lack of experience in playing football, Leslie, who was also trying out, threw a ball to me in a slow easy curve. I managed to catch it and started to run when another fellow tackled me. I fell awkwardly forward. We were not wearing any protective gear, which the coach would shortly ask us to put on before the real tryouts began. I arose from the fall with substantial discomfort in my left shoulder, but still was very anxious to participate. As soon as the coach arrived, we all put on the protective shoulder guard and helmet as per his instructions. Teams were chosen at random and a game started. By this time my shoulder hurt so much that tears formed. The coach, noting my unnatural pose inquired: "What is the matter?" I briefly described my fall. He took one look at my shoulder and ordered me to go to the school nurse. She immediately diagnosed my injury as a broken collar bone.

With my uncle's medical skill, the bone was reset. My shoulder and arm were immobilized by being taped in place with broad bands of adhesive tape. I was of course unable to play football or any other sport for a number of weeks and thus missed the opportunity to become a member of any of the New York Mills football teams. I never did try out for football again.

Werner in New York Mills

Chapter 12

War, Vineland and New York

While I was becoming an American, the war in Europe turned progressively worse. Germany realized that a frontal attack on France through their common border along the Rhein River would be difficult because the massive French defensive structure called the Maginot Line was practically impenetrable. France also assumed that its northern border with Belgium was safe because Belgium was on friendly terms with France. In 1940, Hitler's army, however, surprised the French by launching a lightning fast attack with heavy armor and dive bombers on Holland and Belgium. Their defenses collapsed almost immediately, and Hitler's army proceeded to invade France from the poorly defended northern border

With almost two thousand tanks leading the way, Hitler's Blitzkrieg (lightning war) succeeded beyond anyone's expectations. Within a month the German army had driven the bulk of the French army and the supporting British army onto a sliver of land along the Atlantic Ocean near the city of Dunkurk. About 350,000 British and 100,000 French troops were in a desperate situation from which they were rescued by an emergency flotilla made up of every conceivable British civilian and military ship and boat. The potentially stranded troops were brought to England. The evacuation fleet included private yachts, smaller privately owned pleasure boats, commercial fishing vessels, cargo ships and every ship the British navy could get to the site in a hurry. Over 100,000 tanks, trucks and other vehicles had to be abandoned. The remainder of the French army disintegrated. This disaster ranks with the greatest calamities that ever befell the British army and was the absolute low point of the war. This was June 1940.

Sensing a quick victory, the Italian dictator, Mussolini, declared that Italy would join Germany in the war. France was now under Hitler's control as was almost all of western Europe. What a catastrophe! Dark clouds indeed!

During these dark days, the plight of Jews in Germany worsened steadily, affecting my grandmother, uncle, aunt, and cousin on my mother's side of the family. We heard rumors that Jews were being rounded up and put into brutally run labor camps, but we were somehow reluctant to believe that.

Meanwhile, in our immediate family, our debt to the Eliases of more than three hundred dollars for the ship passage was paramount in impelling my mother to seek employment, which she did as soon as she could speak enough English to make herself understood. With Uncle Mor's help, she obtained a position as nursemaid to a baby of a very wealthy family, where she would also help in the kitchen. She received room and board and six dollars a week. One day each week she had time off to visit us at the Elias home. She then proudly paid three dollars toward retiring the debt and placed two dollars into a bank account intended for the creation of our future home, wherever that might be. Subtracting the car fare for the visit left her less than a dollar a week for her personal needs and clothing.

Inge took several jobs as babysitter for various friends and acquaintances of the Eliases and also did substantial babysitting for the Matt family, who owned the Utica Club Brewing Company. She received a standard fifty-cent payment for each night's sitting. I had my paper route and the mowing jobs in the summer, and I jumped at any other opportunity to earn money. We both deposited some of our earnings in the bank, retaining just enough to pay for our expenses. For me these included paying off the bicycle loan, scout dues of five cents per week, occasional movies at 25 cents admission, haircuts at 35 cents, and sometimes buying a model kit or indulging in some other frivolous but minor expenditure. At periodic intervals, we proudly showed our bank books to Mama, who praised us and encouraged us to save so that someday we could reestablish our family as a unit. This was not only her goal, but also Inge's and mine.

In the fall of 1940, Mother had to decide whether to go with her employer to Florida for the winter or quit her job. By now she was quite attached to the baby in her care, and a new job was not so easy to come by. She thought much about the choice and ended up deciding to go along to Florida for the winter season, leaving Inge and me in Elias' care.

Mother had another motive that influenced her decision. Uncle Mor had done about all he could afford to do by giving Inge and me free room and board, forwarding transit money, and putting money in escrow for the affidavit as well as by taking care of numerous other expenses of ours. Medical practice at that time was nowhere near as lucrative as it is today. To ask Uncle Mor for more money to get Mother's family members out of Germany was just not practical. Yet, Mother constantly had on her mind her mother, Oma Rosa, her brother Walter, his wife Klara, and cousin Gerd, all of whom were still in Germany desperately looking for a way to get out. Mother had approached her employer about the possibility of an affidavit (funds put in escrow for the immigrants as security against their needs), and there seemed to be a good degree of sympathy but no quick response. Time was of the essence since conditions in Germany and Europe were continuously deteriorating according to the sporadic information available to us.

Aside from France having fallen to the Germans and the forced evacuation of the British at Dunkurk, Hungary and Rumania had joined the war on the German side. On top of that, Hitler's Luft Waffe commenced heavy bombing of England in an attempt to force England to surrender without the need for an invasion. In this "Battle of Britain," the English, with relatively few fighter planes, tried desperately to stop the German bombers. As the situation in Europe was changing radically, it worsened for Jews in Germany. The news reports confirmed the sporadic information regarding increasingly extreme measures against German Jews and those in lands under German control. Yellow Star of David badges had to be worn by Jews to permit their instant identification. Their food allowances were repeatedly cut, and the number of stores permitting Jews to enter continuously decreased. Many Jews were expelled from their living quarters. Worst of all there was no communication with Jews under Germany's control, and no news was definitely not good news. Time worked against any effort to get Jews out of Germany in the late months of 1940, but "death camps" were still not in our minds.

It became part of our routine that summer to follow the news broadcasts from England by Edward Murrow who reported that London was burning but that the undaunted fighter pilots of the Royal Air Force were braving the odds and shooting down German aircraft. More than 2,500 German bombers had been shot down by the summer of 1940.

During this time, Mother hoped to obtain the necessary documents from her employer to rescue Uncle Walter, Aunt Klara, Gerd, and Oma Rosa. However, he was procrastinating about supplying the necessary guarantee. In Florida, he discussed the matter with his priest, who pointed out that Germany might well win the war, putting him in an awkward position as a helper of Jews. He finally decided to play it safe and not supply the affidavit, thus shattering my mother's hope.

Although she was in perhaps the most luxurious spot in the United States, the exclusive island of Hobe Sound near Boca Raton in Florida, her stay there became sheer agony.

After the failed attempt to save her mother, brother and family, she could hardly face her employer. A further thorn in her existence in Hobe Sound was that, as the only white servant in that household, she was instructed not to attempt to socialize with the many black servants. With difficulty, she waited to come back north where she quit her job, even though there were few opportunities for other jobs. Thus, she came back to live with the Eliases.

The Elias family socialized primarily with fellow immigrants from Hamburg. These friends did not live in New York Mills but in neighboring towns such as Utica and Rome. Sundays were often spent in nearby scenic parks where the group met to picnic, hike, exchange gossip and discuss the news. One family in the group was the Mengers. They had an extremely precocious daughter, Susie, who was cousin Mark's age and enjoyed playing with him. Years later, as an adult she became a very famous actor's agent in Hollywood.

Mor's best friend was Doctor Hyman, an extroverted bachelor. He was the opposite of Mor both physically and in mental outlook. He was large, rotund, gregarious and cheerfully optimistic; a man who really enjoyed life. Another family in the circle, the Dales, lived in nearby Rome where they had a fur store. It was a mom and pop operation, but the store clientele had grown enough so that they were ready to take on some help. Since Mother was unemployed and had some experience in retail sales as well as being an amateur seamstress, Oscar Dale offered to teach her the fur finishing profession and pay her a very small salary. "Fur finishing" means cutting and sewing the lining into fur coats. She applied herself, and Oscar was happy with her progress but was not in a financial position to give her a raise.

For most of 1941, life in New York Mills was fairly uneventful. Inge and I went to school, walked home to the Elias house for lunch, after which she and I washed and dried the dishes for the whole family, and then rushed back to school. Sundays I did my paper deliveries. Spring to fall and especially summer vacations were the time for me to do mowing and gardening. I had one week of vacation at Scout Camp, where I had a wonderful time. In most of my remaining free time I socialized with my friends. Our hangout was a small candy and grocery shop where we indulged ourselves by each purchasing a pint of chocolate milk that would be consumed very slowly as we gossiped and played checkers or simple card games. Leslie and the others sometimes asked me about my life in Germany. They seemed to be impressed by the diversity of my background and more jealous than sympathetic. For boys accustomed to the humdrum routine of life in the small community of New York Mills, war in England, Kinder transport and Kristall Nacht all seemed to be adventures they would have liked to experience as long as they, like myself, would survive them physically unharmed.

When the Eliases went on weekend outings, Inge and I took turns joining them. The one not going along had the chore of minding the telephone. Since there were no such things as telephone answering machines, we had to take calls and write down messages for the doctor. There were usually several, and Uncle Mor attended to them as soon as he got back home.

Life in the "isolated" United States was relatively peaceful while the war raged in Europe. The Germans overran the Balkan countries, and with little to stop the German juggernaut, England's position became more desperate. America tried to help within the limits imposed by our neutrality. President Roosevelt arranged to trade fifty World War I vintage destroyers to England to help defend against submarines, in exchange for British military bases in the Western Hemisphere. Congress also passed the "Lend-Lease" program to supply urgently needed aid to England. In late June of that year, Germany took the fatal step of invading Russia. That suddenly made the Communist empire of the East an ally of England and a friend of the United States. Well, sort of a friend. Here, the proverb "The enemy of my enemy is my friend" is apropos.

However, the big shocker in 1941 came over the radio on December 7. Japan bombed Pearl Harbor! Thousands of Americans died in that surprise attack on the U.S. fleet located on the Hawaiian Island of Oahu. The next day President Roosevelt addressed the stunned nation on radio—"A date which will live in infamy and will be remembered forever!"

The United States declared war on Japan. Germany then declared war on the United States, who in turn declared war on Germany. The war was now truly a World War.

In the spring of 1942, a shock hit us closer to home. The Stahls, after arriving in the United States, had gone to Baltimore to stay with the Simons. Not too long afterward, Sigmund Stahl enrolled in a school for prospective chicken farmers run by a Jewish help agency. The intent of the school was to retrain immigrants for an enterprise that would permit them to become self- sufficient. He soon purchased a chicken farm in Vineland, New Jersey.

After helping her parents get settled, Ilse Stahl found a job in a dry cleaning store. Because of limited public transportation, Sigmund drove and picked up Ilse each day. One day, as she ran across the street to his waiting car, she was struck and killed by an oncoming automobile. It was a terrible loss, this wonderful young person at age 23. Ilse was as close as one can get to a perfect person. She was not only very attractive but was kindhearted, cheerful, outgoing and helpful to everyone, especially her family. She was a loving daughter admired by everyone who came in contact with her. And now she was gone.

Nanny and Sigmund were understandably devastated and virtually unable to cope with this sudden tragedy. After the funeral, Mother felt that she could do more good trying to help them than she could by maintaining her nominal job in Rome, New York. So she moved in with the Stahls. Mom's positive attitude and physical help was just what was needed to keep the farm going. She got along well with Nanny and Sigmund, and soon she was indispensable.

When the school year ended, she and the Stahls agreed that I should join them in Vineland. I would be closer to the mother I longed for. I would be a good helper to Uncle Sigmund, who was interested in enhancing and enlarging the farm so as to make a little better living.

In June 1942, I arrived in Vineland. The house there had two bedrooms, a living room, a dining room and a kitchen on the first floor. My room was a small dormer room in the attic. I soon became very involved with Uncle Sigmund operating and improving the farm. Both of us were amateurs, but we worked cooperatively and tried to learn from friends and neighbors and even more so from our own experiences. That summer we started the enlargement program by fencing several acres of grazing land at the back of the property. This fenced-in area could now be used to hold young pullets. We became adept at manually digging post holes and stretching and securing the wire mesh fence to posts. We built summer shelters for the young pullets, who roamed freely until fall. One-week-old baby chicks were normally purchased early in spring. Within about eight weeks they were ready to be put out to pasture as young pullets. By fall, when they were about six months old and starting to lay eggs, they were called hens and were put into chicken coops. We dug ditches for water pipes for the chickens on the range and built a dog house for the mongrel dog we acquired. His primary function was to guard the pullets from foxes and other predators. The dog loved to bark but was really very friendly. He soon became my pet. He was quite clever.

Somehow he succeeded in having a chicken that started to lay eggs come into his doghouse and lay the egg there. He would then gently tap the egg until the shell broke, then he licked up this delicacy, leaving only the telltale shell fragments.

Early every morning we inspected all twenty chicken coops, looking for anything out of the ordinary, such as an occasional dead chicken. We cleaned their automated water trays and fed the chickens. Every day with the assistance of Mama and Nanny, we collected eggs and cleaned them with sandpaper. Cleaning eggs with water would deteriorate their quality. After cleaning, we sorted the eggs by weight (pee wee, small, medium, large and jumbo). Then we checked for internal blood spots by candling and packed them into crates of 30 dozen per crate. We brought the crates to a cooperative auction where they were sold in bulk. We averaged close to 3000 eggs a day, seven days a week, and every egg was hand processed, a seemingly unending job.

We periodically cleaned the chicken coops. Chickens slept on a raised set of roosts, the underside of which was made of mesh wire so that the chicken droppings would fall through. To remove the chicken droppings, we raised the roost assembly, which was hinged in the back, and the droppings were shoveled out. They were then sold to vegetable farmers for fertilizer.

One reason I enjoyed my work was the camaraderie Uncle Sigmund and I shared. He treated me like an adult and respected my opinions. One hot summer evening after completing the building of a shelter, he said, "Werner, you worked like a man, I want to treat you like a man. Let's go to the tavern down the road and I'll buy you a beer." I had never tasted beer in my life, but I was honored by the offer and accompanied him. He ordered two glasses of beer. I expected it to taste like ginger ale, which it visually resembled. What a disappointment when I took my first sip! I really did not like it at all, but I felt obligated to drink most of it. How could I refuse this kindness and respect?

Vineland had a sizable number of other German Jewish chicken farmers, and friendships between them developed readily, nurtured by their common interests and common religion. We attended religious services in a synagogue having German-style ritual. I became friendly with several young members of the congregation, but real close relationships never developed since school and work had priority, and I never considered myself a permanent Vinelander. I did meet one girl with whom I became quite friendly, Doris Meyer, and when it was time for school to start in the fall, and I enrolled in the Vineland Central High School, she was in my class. She was very bright and eventually became valedictorian. My focus, however, was not yet on girls. One of my elective courses was wood shop. As part of the war effort, we each were to build an accurate scale model of an aircraft. The models would be used for aircraft recognition drills by air force pilots. The models were not constructed from kits, but were produced from scratch as per supplied drawings. At the end of the semester, the models that were sufficiently accurate and sturdy were painted black and given to the army air force. The builder received a certificate of recognition. Many of the students' models were below par and were not accepted by the military even after being touched up by the instructor, but I was fortunate enough to receive two certificates while in school in Vineland. I was extremely proud of my achievement since I completed two planes, both of which were difficult to build. My first model was the Vought F4U Corsair. The main difficulty in constructing that plane was the gull shaped wings. With the aid of the teacher, I first made a jig to enable me to produce the complex wings with proper symmetry. Since I did a good job in good time on the first model, the instructor encouraged me to try a tougher model for my second project, the Curtis SOC Seagull. This was a biplane with a main pontoon and two outrigger pontoons, one of the few biplanes used in World War II. It took me the balance of the semester to complete and its acceptance was the highlight of my school year.

By late fall, the work on the farm had slowed down a bit, and I was urged to get a part-time job after school. A job would permit me to earn some money for myself since money was still very scarce. After school hours, I went to several stores in downtown Vineland and asked to see the manager to inquire whether they might need a stock boy or delivery boy for after the school hours. With each refusal, I became more discouraged. I was so downcast by the repeated refusals that I almost quit trying. Finally, at the Sun Ray Drug Store, the manager, a Mr. Brenner, said he could use me and would pay 25 cents per hour. That was great, and I worked there after school for the rest of my stay in Vineland.

One embarrassing moment occurred shortly after I started to work there. There was an intercom system from the store to the basement stockroom. A request came for a case of Kotex. I picked a case and brought it upstairs and asked one of the salesgirls, "Where do you put these?" She blushed and giggled and walked away while another salesgirl came to my rescue and showed me the counter where feminine hygiene items were sold.

In the fall, my mother also got a job as a fur finisher in the only fur store in Vineland. So finally we were back on the road to saving some money, hoping that we would establish our own family unit again. Inge, meanwhile, had turned 16, stopped attending school and moved to New York City. There she lived with my mother's cousin Erna Strauss and family. Inge had moved to New York City to attend beautician's school so that she might learn a trade. She had saved enough money to attend the Wilfred Beauty Academy. When she graduated, she got a job as a beautician. She was then able to pay for room and board at the Strausses.

By the spring of 1943, the Stahls were pretty much back in control of things. Their farm had been expanded with the addition of the ranges and shelters. They had received a jury award of $1,600 for the loss of Ilse. The Lowensterns, who had scraped together a living in Baltimore, decided to move to Vineland to become chicken farmers like the Stahls.

Now the need on the farm for Mother and me had diminished, and Mother was fairly confident of her fur-finishing skills, so all agreed that the time was right for us to reunite our family. After talking to Inge, and friends and relatives, Mother decided that New York City was where we would relocate. That is where there were a number of people she knew and where there seemed to be the best opportunity for our future. The Manhattan area of New York City called Washington Heights had a heavy concentration of German Jewish immigrants. Here entrepreneurs had developed stores, restaurants as well as social and religious institutions which duplicated the German style we were accustomed to. Some called the area "Frankfurt on the Hudson." That would be our new home. Inge located and rented an apartment in Washington Heights, on west 173rd Street. Our rent was $40 per month for a fifth-floor walkup apartment consisting of two rooms and a bathroom, and kitchen. Mother had calculated that with her and Inge working, we would manage. The plan was for me to follow as soon as Mother had a job and I finished the school year in Vineland.

And so it went. When my school year was over and I finished helping Uncle Sigmund with a few remaining chores, I left by bus for New York City. Uncle Sigmund gave me a farewell gift of twenty dollars in appreciation of my efforts, and off I went. This trip hopefully was the final step in reestablishing our family without the charity of relatives, a goal all three of us had longed for ardently since we separated in the spring of 1939. The bus that took me to New York City terminated at 42nd Street. The recollection I still have of my first impression was that the city appeared to be far more crowded and busier than I thought it would be. Everyone seemed to be dashing about at double speed. I had written instructions stating that I should get to the 8th Avenue subway station where I should get onto the uptown "A" train. I was rather nervous doing this alone. I asked for directions to the subway station and succeeded in getting on the uptown "A" train. Once on the train, as I watched, the next station was 59th Street. Then the train seemed to fly through a number of other stations without stopping. I became a bit alarmed that there might be something wrong. I was relieved when the train stopped at 125th Street. Next it passed through another station before stopping at 145th Street. Apparently the train did not stop at every station. Next came the stop at the 168th Street station. Despite my instructions to exit at 173rd Street, I felt sufficiently panicky and got off at 168th street since 173rd street seemed too close at hand and would probably be bypassed by this train. I got off and looked for an exit to the street. After a little confusion, I figured out the directions of the streets and walked with my suitcase in hand to 173rd Street. Then, checking house numbers, I found my way to the number 720. Full of anticipation, I dashed up the five flights of stairs at a run seemingly without effort.

I rang the bell and with greater happiness than I had experienced in a long time, hugged my mother. Inge would soon come home from work. That evening we all felt very giddy at achieving the goal we had striven for for such a long, long time. In our new home, Mom slept on the couch in the living room, and Inge and I shared the bedroom. Furniture had all been bought secondhand except for a bridge table and four chairs that were purchased new. This table served many purposes, including those of dining table and desk. My clothing was very limited, consisting mostly of hand-me-downs, probably cousin Irving's former clothes sent to us by the Simons. I did have a few items of clothing that Mother had purchased, but they were pretty much threadbare. On our first Saturday in New York, Inge insisted that she and I go to what appeared to me to be a rather upscale men's department store on 181st street, Crawford's, where she treated me to a brand-new pair of light brown slacks and a matching sport shirt. I felt deeply grateful and well dressed in my new togs. How wonderful to be blessed with a fantastic sister like mine!

Upon arriving in New York, Mother immediately set out to find a job. Since her experience, though limited, was that of fur finisher in a retail fur store, she first tried to get a job in one of the local fur stores. This was the summer season however, and hardly the time when fur stores needed help. With the referral of an acquaintance she applied for a job at a fur manufacturing establishment in the down town New York fur district (on 34th street) and was offered a position as a fur operator, sewing fur pelts together. She knew how to operate a sewing machine and quickly adapted to the special type of sewing machine used in the industry. Her place of work was a factory with perhaps twenty employees. Shortly after she started to work there, she inquired if they could use me for the summer as a general helper, and her boss said yes. So, the week after I arrived, I joined her in going to work.

My tasks at my new job became progressively more diversified. I started with sweeping floors and cleaning toilets. Then they showed me how to stretch moistened fur sections and nail them to a board to dry, after which the fur sections would keep their expanded shape. I learned how to touch up Persian fur paws[7] that were poorly colored, having brown streaks. These I touched up using black permanent dye sticks which made them look properly black. I learned how to bundle fur sections that had been matched by a more skilled employee. Occasionally I was asked to deliver completed coats to retail stores. For deliveries I was given the necessary subway fare of 5 cents for each direction of travel. Before long I realized that for deliveries that were not too far away, I could pocket the fare for myself by walking to the destination. That worked fine until one

---

[7] Persian fur paws are small pieces of the fur from Persian lamb's feet.

day it started to rain in the middle of my walking delivery. The brand new coat became a bit wet, even though it was covered by a paper sleeve. I enjoyed the challenges of the work, but by the end of the summer, I was happy to go back to school.

Since I was always intrigued by the romance of flying, I wanted to go to the High School of Aeronautical Trades at La Guardia Airport, but when I went there to enroll, I did not have the necessary prerequisites. At the suggestion of the school guidance counselor, I ended up at George Washington High School in upper Manhattan. The year was 1943. The war had begun to turn against the Germans. The Russian army had stopped the Germans at Stalingrad. The Allies had succeeded in defeating the Germans and Italians in North Africa and had invaded Italy. The U.S. was on a full war footing, and everyone was enthusiastically supporting the war effort. Unlike later wars, during the entire duration of World War II an overwhelmingly strong patriotic fervor permeated the country.

As I enrolled in school, I looked forward to my 18th birthday when I would be eligible to be drafted into the armed services. At school, the curriculum incorporated a blend of patriotic war spirit and academics. I remember an English class where Mrs. Jamerson was our teacher. One of our first homework assignments was to memorize a poem written by an air force pilot; John Gillespie Magee Jr. It was supposedly written on the back of an envelope addressed to his parents. It was his last letter home before he was killed in combat. The poem:

"Oh, I have slipped the surly bonds of earth
and danced the skies in laughter-silvered wings
sunward I've climbed and joined the tumbling mirth
of sun-split clouds—and done a hundred things
you have not dreamed of—wheeled and soared and swung
high in the sunlit silence. Hov'ring there,

I've chased the shouting winds along and flung
my eager craft through footless halls of air.
Up, up the long delirious burning blue
I've topped the wind swept heights with easy grace.
Where never lark, or even eagle flew;
and while with silent lifting mind I've trod
the high untrespassed sanctity of space
Put out my hand, and touched the face of God."

Some days later, Mrs. Jamerson requested a recitation to show that we had memorized the poem as requested. She called on us in alphabetical order. As she called the student's name, he or she was to come to the front of the classroom and recite the poem. She called the first name on her alphabetized roster, "Frank Agiletti." He did not know it. She raised her voice slightly and advised that she had a simple rule: "If you do your homework as required, you get a mark of 100%. If you don't, you get a 0%. Your term grade will be the average of these marks." "Agiletti," she stated, "you have just earned yourself a 0." Next was Joan Brandt. She knew only the first line and likewise earned a 0%. And so down the roster.

While this was happening, I was frantically trying to learn by heart this poem that I too had not memorized. My turn came up near the end of the class session. Nervously, I walked to the front of the classroom and started to rattle off the lines, slurring the words badly. I had managed to memorize only part of the poem. However, she soon stopped me, commenting that apparently I had done my homework, but that I was killing this beautiful poem by my terrible pronunciation. She pointed out that in a previous semester, she had another German refugee student whose diction she had helped to improve. He ended up becoming the valedictorian of the graduating class. (His name was Henry Kissinger.) She identified my mispronunciations and asked me to repeat the poem from the start, slowly and with proper emphasis. Just as I started again, the bell rang, signaling the end of the class session. Not only was I relieved, but a number of students, whose last names followed Neuburger, thanked me for saving them from a 0% mark. I was the hero of the moment.

The next day I, as well as the remaining students who had not been called on, pretty well knew the poem. Throughout that year, Mrs. Jamerson did her best to improve my diction. Not only she, but a classmate, Millie Grau, took an interest in me. Millie became my very good friend, and I did not mind at all having an attractive girl trying to help me in many ways. Another friendship I developed was with my classmate, Frank Grunebaum. Frank joined me in taking an extracurricular course called Navigational Computation offered by the math department. We took this optional course in the hope that it might be of advantage to us once we got into the armed service. Our dream was to become pilots. Aside from this optional course, I finished all the required courses so as to be qualified to graduate in June of 1944.

Prior to graduation, the senior prom was held. I was reluctant to go, but Frank convinced me to get Millie as my date and join him and his girlfriend. After extensive procrastination I screwed up my courage and asked Millie. I had, alas, waited too long and had given too many negative signals. She would have liked to go with me, but since I did not ask her earlier she had accepted the offer from another boy.

Now that Frank had convinced me to go, I asked another classmate, Elaine Seilman. She was happy to be asked. So we were all set, except that neither Frank nor I knew how to dance. Frank, being more worldly, decided we'd take a crash course at the Arthur Murray dance studio. We went there, explaining our predicament: that we had only two weeks before the prom to learn to dance. A sympathetic female teacher suggested that we take two lessons, which would cost us ten dollars. She tried to teach us two clumsy oafs, and we ended up mastering the basic box step, which would work for most dances. In those days, the main dances were the fox trot, the waltz and the rumba. The jitterbug was considered inappropriate for a formal dance and more exotic dances like the tango were seldom played. Thus, we confidently proceeded to rent tuxedos and buy corsages for the most formal event in our lives so far. The prom was a success, and we ended the evening at the then famous Billy Rose's Diamond Horseshoe night club. I felt as though I had tasted the forbidden fruit of American materialism in its most intoxicating form.

Frank and I remained friends for many years. Millie was upset that I had not asked her earlier. As a consolation, I asked her to go to the movies downtown. This was to be my first date alone with a girl. We saw *The Story of Dr. Wassel* at the Rivoly Theater. It was Sunday, June 11, 1944, five days after the Allies had landed in Normandy, France.

While in school, I had obtained a job in a fruit and vegetable store near the corner of Broadway and 181st Street, Joe Green's Fruit Market. I worked there from 6 to 10 o'clock on weekday evenings and on Saturday when the store was open until midnight. The reason for the late Saturday hours was to take advantage of any customers passing the store after the last showing of the films in the Coliseum movie house across the street. When the movie let out, there was usually a small rush of customers. Afterward, we would pull the movable fruit display stands into the store and lock up the gates.

There were three workers at night: an older, more experienced man, a full-time apprentice, Angelo Tzardakas and myself. Angelo was of Greek descent but born in the U.S. He and I became good friends. After work we often rode our bicycles, coasting downhill on Broadway from 181st Street to 192nd Street. There we then waited for a streetcar going back. We then held onto the rear of the streetcar so that it would pull us back up the hill. Because of the war, unlike today, there were few cars on the road. Gasoline was rationed, and most men were in the military service. Women did not drive cars as much as today, so at night the streets were practically empty of automobiles. Our bicycle riding on Broadway was relatively safe. It was only the ride hitching onto the streetcar that was somewhat treacherous.

I graduated from high school in 1944. Thereafter Angelo and I decided to go on a bicycle trip, and we selected Niagara Falls as our destination. Our choice was strongly influenced by the fact that Millie's family had a summer home in Copake, New York, where she was staying for the summer. That would be our destination for the first night based on Millie's invitation to visit and my anxiousness to see her again.

We started out with twenty dollars each and a small bundle of spare underwear and socks and a raincoat, all fitted into a soft bag, tied to the carrier platform above the rear wheel. A prior one-day test ride to Bedford and Mount Kisco and back home— a trip of about 60 miles—led us to believe that we could average about 80 miles per day. That rate of travel should allow us to reach Niagara Falls in five to six days. We'd then either cycle home, or if we were too tired, or if it took us much longer to get there, we'd take the train home. We checked into the train fare, which was less than seven dollars each plus two dollars for each bicycle. With the anticipated cost of one dollar per day for food, we thought we should make it as planned. As for sleeping, we planned to sleep under the stars. Mama did not fully comprehend the extent of our plans, so I was able to get her permission.

And so we started our excursion. The bicycles had balloon tires, and in those days there were no shiftable gears on bikes. Hence, hills became real challenges. We started early in the morning and reached Route 22 near the city of White Plains, which we followed all the way to Copake. At noon we reached Brewster, about 50 miles into our trip, but then the route became very hilly. Our legs began to ache. We became fatigued, but felt that we were committed to Copake and kept encouraging each other and pedaling until almost 9 P.M. when we reached our destination. The sun had already set. We had traveled more than 100 miles and were more than exhausted. Millie and her family had expected us much earlier and were quite concerned. We were so weary and frazzled that all we could do was eat a little bit and fall asleep. The next morning we reevaluated our plan and came to the conclusion that our distances were too ambitious, so we traveled only about 60 miles that day past Amsterdam, New York. We stopped when we discovered some abandoned cabins along Route 5. In what apparently once was a clearing in a wooded area, now overgrown with scrub growth, there were perhaps ten cabins, some of which had collapsed but several were still standing. Each cabin was a one-room facility which once had a kitchenette and bathroom. Even in the cabins still standing, only remnants of these facilities remained. They apparently were once used, somewhat like motels, but low tourist traffic due to the war had caused these, like many other cabin colonies throughout the country, to be abandoned. We decided to take advantage of the primitive but free shelter, selected the least decrepit cabin, and had a reasonably good night's rest.

The third day we reached Utica. The Eliases no longer lived there. Uncle Mor had joined the army as a doctor and was stationed at an army camp in the South where Aunt Else and Mark had joined him. I made a phone call to say hello to Uncle Mor's friend, Doctor Hyman, whom I remembered well from my stay in New York Mills. He invited us to sleep over for the night. He was very cordial, and when he inquired about our plans and finances, he generously gave Angelo and me each a five dollar bill to reinforce our precarious finances.

With replenished funds and refreshed spirit, we moved along toward Rochester. This was our fourth day, and we splurged by renting a room for the night at a charge of one dollar each. In those days it was common for private homeowners to offer rooms for rent, much like motels do today. Motels as we know them now did not exist. Aside from hotels, the closest thing to a motel was a cabin for rent, but cabins, although cheaper than hotels, were more expensive than rooms and were generally rented for more than one night.

For food, we typically bought a quart of milk (for 10 cents), a loaf of white bread (for another 10 cents), and a jar of peanut butter or jelly (for about 20 cents). That was our breakfast. We ate the leftover bread and spread for lunch. Water served as our lunch beverage. Evenings we stopped at a diner for soup and some other inexpensive item. (Soup was 25 cents for a large bowl.)

The fifth day we rolled along Route 18, skirting the southern shore of Lake Ontario and eventually reached the outskirts of Niagara Falls. By this time we had resolved that we would take the train home, giving us an extra day at the falls. We spent the next day at Niagara Falls, looking at the falls from several points of view, but because I was not a United States citizen we dared not go to the Canadian side. We walked onto Luna and Goat Islands and along the river edge and were duly impressed, but were so tired that we went to bed early that night in a room we had rented. The next morning we took one last look at the plunging falls, let the mist of the falls hit our faces, and then went to the railroad station to buy our tickets for home.

The trip home was like a real vacation. We sat in the fairly empty train, our feet propped up on the empty seats across from us, jokingly complimenting each other on how well we were now moving without pedaling. I also remember our commenting on the beauty of the landscape, which now past by us so much faster than when we were laboriously pedaling along on our bikes. The trip home seemed to take no time at all, and our families as well as our boss, Joe Green, were happy to see us back home safe and sound.

Chapter 13

This Is the Army

When I turned eighteen on September 7, 1944, I registered for the draft. Though required to register by law, I was very anxious to do so. The war was proceeding well for the Allies by that time. Rumania, which previously had joined Germany as an ally, and Bulgaria, which had tried not to get involved, both now declared war on Germany. Allied forces had broken out of Normandy and were advancing across France. Paris had been liberated on August 25, and Allied troops had landed in southern France. Allied bombers were blasting Axis military and industrial targets. In the Pacific, American forces had captured Guam and Saipan and had landed on Guadalcanal. In the Philippine Islands, General MacArthur had returned to Leyte Island. These victories, however, came at a very high cost of life.

Despite the heavy losses, Americans were united as never thereafter, and possibly never before, in their resolve to destroy the evil empires of Germany and Japan. The press, radio, the movies, schools, politicians, Boy Scouts and other civic organizations all encouraged the patriotism that permeated the country. By this time I harbored a burning hatred for Germans, and I was anxious to do what I could to help in the war effort. I was afraid I might miss being in the war if victorious combat continued at this pace; hence I was anxiously awaiting my induction. In the meantime, I worked a full-time day shift at Joe Green's fruit and vegetable market. At that market, customers looked at me askance. "Why aren't you in the military service?" they would brazenly ask. I generally responded that I was classified 1A and was anxiously waiting for my induction. Yes, the general spirit of patriotism and service was unlike any other time I can remember. During that time I also enrolled at City College of New York as a night student taking two courses. These were subjects I liked, Mechanical Drafting and Mathematics. On weekends I would go to the movies and occasionally the opera with Millie. Sometimes we double dated with Frank Grunebaum and his girlfriend Karen.

Finally, on November 29, I received my classification: 1A— "physically fit, acceptable for general military service." I was delighted, because to be anything other than 1A would have been very embarrassing and even disgraceful to me. Many young men were ashamed to admit it if they were rejected for military service. Now I was impatient for my induction orders, which finally arrived on January 10, 1945. My induction orders read as follows:

> *From the president of the United States to Werner Neuburger, Order #12819, Greetings: Having submitted yourself to a local board composed of your neighbors for the purpose of determining your availability for training and service in the land and naval forces of the United States, you are hereby notified that you have now been selected for training and service therein. You will therefore report to the local board named above at 3785 Broadway (Room 10) at 7.00 A.M. on the 30th day of January 1945.*

Mother accompanied me, and while not quite as enthusiastic as I was, she was very proud indeed. In conversation with some of my new fellow recruits, I soon discovered that several were of German Jewish descent while the others were mostly native born Americans. I soon struck up a friendship with two of the new German Jewish recruits, Seymour Weill and Eric Rogger (formerly his name was Rosenfeld). We remained good buddies throughout our basic training. From 3785 Broadway, we were taken to an induction station near Grand Central Terminal, downtown. Here, we were processed and solemnly sworn to allegiance. I received my army serial number: 42205056. Together with many other new recruits, we boarded the army bus to Fort Dix where we were further processed in a more military manner and outfitted with military clothing. We were instructed to ship all our civilian clothing back home—shoes, underwear and even handkerchiefs. Henceforth, we were not allowed to wear any clothing other than that which was issued to us. Hence, the term *GI* (government issue).

We were issued underwear, handkerchiefs, socks, one dress shirt, one pair of pants, one dress jacket, one cap—all colored olive drab (OD). We also received a tan shirt, tie, pants and cap. In addition we each received two pairs of fatigues consisting of pants, jacket, hat and leggings. The latter would be our daily work clothing. Further, we were given a wool sleeping bag and a duffel bag, both olive drab. Finally we received one pair of boots, a pistol belt with accessories, a regular belt, and a lightweight poncho. The poncho served as a raincoat as well as a shelter half. Two shelter halves would snap together to make a pup tent big enough for two. The pistol belt was a 3-inch-wide, heavy-duty web belt with eyelets to hold a canteen, a first aid kit, bayonet and ammunition pouches.

Loaded down with all this new clothing and gear, we struggled to proceed to a checkout station where the fit of our newly issued clothing was crudely confirmed. If clothing was within one or two sizes of a proper fit, it was considered acceptable.

The next morning we were shown how to stencil our serial number on every one of our items. We received a long series of lectures, including a heavy dose of instructions on army discipline and military behavior. We were read the entire articles of war (the military rules and regulations). Then more lectures and instructions on how to stow all our new stuff into the duffel bag. The next day we boarded a train that would bring us to our basic training camp. We all wondered where we were going and were pleasantly surprised when the rumor of Florida was confirmed.

Our destination was Camp Blanding near Jacksonville, Florida. There, we were assigned to the 219th Infantry Training Battalion. Each of us was issued an M1 rifle and a bayonet, a backpack, an entrenching tool, a mess kit, a steel helmet and plastic helmet liner, a compass, and a gas mask. There might have been other items, but I do not remember them.

Next we were led to our quarters, a two-story barrack. Each floor contained a dormitory with about twenty cots, a communal bathroom, and a barrack chief's room. We were each assigned a cot, an adjacent foot locker and a shelf with hooks where we placed our rifles, gas masks, backpacks, entrenching tools and dress clothing. We stowed all other possessions except the boots in the foot locker. Nothing else was allowed to be visible.

A very rugged 15 weeks of training began. We learned how to make our beds, army style. The bottom of the bed sheet was folded under the mattress: then the overhanging sides were folded at 45 degrees and tightly tugged in. The same with the blanket. Then the top sheet was folded back onto the blanket to show exactly one hand's width (4") of white. When done properly, a half dollar coin[8] dropped onto the blanket would bounce.

---

[8] In those days half-dollar pieces were common coinage. Today they are no longer in circulation.

Everything in the foot locker had to be neatly folded. We had frequent inspections. A poorly made bed, a messy foot locker or dust anywhere would lead to extra duty. To me the least desirable extra duty was K.P. (kitchen police). You had to get up at 4 A.M. to help prepare breakfast in the company kitchen then work in the kitchen all day until it was spotlessly clean after the evening meal. K.P. thus usually meant a 16-hour day without much of a break. Some of us were unfortunate to have more K.P. than we felt we deserved. I had the feeling, shared by my New York City compatriots, that the cadre was slightly biased against the New York City slickers, or maybe their bias was against Jews? My buddy, Seymour Weill, who often served K.P. with me, took full advantage of this adversity of having K.P. by cozying up to the mess sergeant. Seymour liked being in the kitchen, and at the end of the basic training he was successful in being transferred to cooking school. His philosophy was that if he worked in the kitchen, he would never go hungry. Our company was a mix of recruits from Pennsylvania, Ohio, Arkansas, New Jersey and New York. The recruits from each state initially tended to associate with each other, but friendships soon transcended this restraint and developed based on compatible personalities. However, above and beyond any clannishness, we developed a team spirit that minimized any geographic or other differences. The first Saturday was a training day, but the next day, Sunday, was a day off. A number of the men expressed their intention to go to church and invited me and another fellow who happened to be Jewish to join them. When we explained that we were Jewish, they expressed surprise. We seemed to them like regular guys. There might have been some feelings of prejudice, but I never sensed any religious intolerance and found myself more the object of curiosity than dislike. The curiosity may have been fueled by my accent, but I recall no negative incidents. The fact that I was of German origin only created an affinity with several men whose grandparents or great grandparents had come from Germany a long time ago. The fact that some of us were Jewish and of German descent did not create any friction or animosity that I noticed. Essentially we were all in the same subordinate position—we were recruits. This tolerance may seem utopian, but that is how I clearly remember it.

We experienced discipline not only in the barracks but on every event of the day. Any shortcoming during training could easily lead to Sunday K.P., Sunday being the only day normally free. We trained six days a week from early morning until suppertime, and frequently trained at night.

We trained as a team in an organized system. Our basic unit was a squad consisting of 10 men led by a training corporal. Three squads constituted a platoon led by a sergeant and a second lieutenant. A platoon thus had 30 trainees. Three platoons constituted a company, 90 trainees, commanded by a first lieutenant. Each company was a fairly self-contained unit, with its own administrative group, quartermaster and mess hall with kitchen. The entire company was headed by a captain, aided by a first sergeant. Three companies, roughly 375 men, constituted our training battalion. It was explained to us that upon completion of infantry training that we would be split up to become replacements for casualties in actual combat units.

What did this training consist of? The first eight weeks we learned to form up, march in step, position the rifle on command, run in step and salute just about everything that was moving. Saluting was required whenever you faced or passed an officer, any officer, anywhere, in camp or outside of camp, while on duty or on furlough. And within our training confines we also had to salute our training noncoms, the sergeants. Every day we had calisthenics including such squad activities as lifting a telephone pole horizontally and tossing it to another squad. We marched, often twenty miles per day, with rifle weighing about eight pounds, and wearing our steel helmet. Both seemed to get heavier by the hour. The field packs (backpack with entrenching tool and mess kit plus other items) on our backs just added to the "joy." We learned to dig fox holes, which were about three feet in diameter and three to four feet deep, big enough for one person to get into and be completely below the ground. The foxhole had to be dug well enough so that it would not collapse if a tank rode over it, and everyone's foxhole was put to that test. We trained to crawl through mud and ditches and under barbed wire while live ammunition was shot above us. Yes, the army was toughening us up.

We learned how to use a compass and read a map so as to be able to patrol a specified course. The final test of that training exercise turned out rather badly. A team of three of us was given an assignment to reach a designated location. To get there we had to use our compass. We sighted on a fixed object in the distance and counted the steps, which averaged about two feet each, until we got to the selected spot. We then repeated the procedure for the next leg of our course. At one point we aligned our sight on a distant brown object visible through the fairly dense forest. When we came closer to the brown object, it turned out to be a cow walking across our path. This leg of our course threw us off the proper path so that we did not get to our destination until a rescue team found us and guided us there. Most embarrassing!

We were taught how to take a rifle apart and put it back together, and before long we could and did it blindfolded. We learned how to shoot standing, kneeling and prone on the ground. Early on, I realized that the M1 rifle was designed for right-hand operation. The left hand normally supports the forward part of the rifle, while the right hand pulls back on the bolt handle (located on the right side of the rifle). This action loads a bullet by transferring it from the magazine into the firing chamber. The right hand is then placed on the trigger. Since my eyesight is poor in my right eye, I had to hold the rifle against my left shoulder in order to align the target sight with my left eye. Pulling back the bolt was awkward, and so was positioning my right hand on the trigger.

I explained my problem to the sergeant at the rifle range. He smiled like a Cheshire cat, expressing questionable sympathy, and asked whether I wanted a left-handed rifle. That sounded perfectly sensible to me and I said, "Yes, sir." He advised me that I would need to get my platoon sergeant's permission. I proceeded to do so at my first opportunity, only to be told to get permission from the company commander. This would be my first personal confrontation with such a high-ranking officer. I was reluctant but I felt a sufficient need to proceed.

When we returned from the firing range, I proceeded to company headquarters where the first sergeant barked at me, inquiring what I wanted. In my best military manner, I stood at attention, saluted smartly, and stated my request. He softened his tone a bit and told me to wait while he checked with the captain. Returning shortly, he stated that the captain wanted to see me. Trying to keep calm, I entered the holy sanctuary of the captain's office. Here sat the company commander behind his busy desk, looking every bit as awesome as I feared he might look. Too late now! I again saluted smartly and stated my request. The captain looked at me for what seemed like an eternity. It probably was no more than five seconds. Then he simply told me to check with the supply sergeant, to see if he had any left-handed rifles in stock. I said, "Thank you, SIR." I saluted, executed a military about face, and exited. I went to the supply sergeant as ordered. Again, I saluted as I approached his desk and confidently restated my request. He, not having the same finesse as the others, broke into a laugh which confirmed what I had begun to suspect: there are no left-handed rifles. I was being sent on a fool's errand. I retreated with as much dignity as I could muster and joined my fellow trainees as if nothing happened.

We learned not only to shoot rifles but also machine guns, bazookas, mortars, Browning automatic rifles (BAR's), carbines, submachine guns, and rifle grenades. We learned how to throw hand grenades and set booby traps. We trained and learned and learned and trained and were continually advised that before long our lives would depend on what we learned.

At the end of the first eight intensive weeks of basics, we were divided into specialty groups: line rifle men including sharpshooters (snipers), light and heavy machine gunners, thirty and sixty mm mortar men, and cannoneers. Because I had some math aptitude, I was assigned to a cannon company. A cannon company, although equipped with 105 mm cannons, is part of the infantry, not the artillery. Infantry cannons are of lighter weight construction than artillery units and thus more mobile. To set the height and azimuth (horizontal direction), one had to read a vernier.[9] Our cannon fired shells about four inches in diameter (105 millimeters) and about 18 inches long. It was the heaviest weapon used by the infantry. Heavier 105 mm howitzers (having longer barrels) and weapons that shot 155 mm and 240 mm ammunition are the domain of the field artillery. By the way, there is a difference between a gun and a rifle. A gun has a smooth barrel interior. A rifle barrel had a series of interior spiral grooves which cause the ammunition to rotate as it is propelled out of the barrel, increasing its accuracy, much like a football.

As members of a cannon company, we had to learn how to manually move the gun into position, how to aim, and how to correct the aim so that we hit the target within three shots. The good thing about being a cannoneer was that we got to learn how to drive the vehicles that pulled the cannons. These vehicles were called 6 by 6s. They were larger than a jeep but smaller than a full-sized truck.

The first part of our driver training consisted of stop-and-go driving on a blacktop field. The hard part was that shifting gears required double clutching. There were no automatic transmissions, and the sound of grinding gears was grounds for disqualification. More by luck than skill, I managed to keep the

---

[9] Vernier is a small measuring device used to obtain fine adjustment.

vehicle moving reasonably smoothly. Those who qualified were challenged to drive the 6 by 6 through fields and on rutty roads. The next day the men who had qualified had to drive with a cannon hitched to the rear of the 6 by 6. We went through the same maneuvers plus the most challenging task, backing the cannon into a specified spot.

After qualifying I received my blue card (military driver's license) and became quite expert at the tasks required of us. After we finished the full course of training, I and about 50 others, out of a battalion of about 300 trainees, received an award, the Expert Infantry Badge. The best part of this award was that it entitled us to a five dollar per month increase in our salary which was twenty-one dollars per month. That doesn't sound like much today, but we really didn't need much money since everything—that is clothing, food and shelter—was provided. Our pay was used mainly for playing poker, an occasional movie (25 cents admission), and buying beer and ice cream and personal items at the post exchange (PX), where everything was sold at a substantial discount. Postage was free, and I spent much of my free evening time writing to family and friends. Despite being constantly surrounded by fellow trainees, it was very easy to feel lonely and to long for home.

By the end of basic training, we had developed real camaraderie. As some of the training graduates were immediately sent overseas as replacements in combat units, we were truly sorry to be separated. Fortunately, the tide of war in Europe had turned in our favor. On the eastern front, the Russian army was advancing into Germany and Austria. The allies with overwhelming superiority of war materials and numbers of troops were likewise advancing on the western front. It would not be much longer before the German military machine, faced with huge losses, disintegrated completely. In the Pacific, however, the bloody battle of Iwo Jima was in full swing; there the war there was far from over.

I and a few others were sent to Camp Maxey near the town of Paris, Texas, for a few weeks of advanced training, consisting mostly of bivouac and various cannon maneuvers. Here, we learned how to clear woods so cannon could be fired while being concealed, to ready cannons to fire after traveling through water, and to keep them properly maintained under all kinds of circumstances.

While in the field, three members of our company were called to the commander's tent and told that we, together with all the other trainees in our group, were scheduled to go overseas soon. But since the three of us were not citizens, we would become citizens now. We were to travel to Paris, Texas, for the proceedings. Paris was about 60 miles away. He asked who had an army driver's license. Unwittingly, I moved my hand; he declared that I was accepted as a volunteer and that I was to drive the company jeep.

I was nervous, unsure of how to drive the jeep. I had never driven a jeep before, and my total driving experience added up to maybe four hours. To make things worse; we had to travel over very rough terrain until we got to the paved road. Once we were on our way, I tried several times to shift from first to second gear, but somehow the double clutching (clutch engagement and shifting to neutral, then releasing and engaging clutch again to shift to second gear, then releasing clutch), caused me either to stall or grind the gears. Since I didn't want to ruin the jeep's transmission and none of the other fellows were willing to drive, I drove all the way to Paris in first gear.

Somewhat delayed because of the slow speed of travel, we arrived at the courthouse where a brief but poignant ceremony converted us from aliens to citizens. The judge congratulated us individually and wished us well. I was extremely relieved when we got back to our unit because I feared that driving such a long distance in first gear might burn out the engine. If we had gotten stuck, we had no telephone or even a telephone number to get help.

The next week we were told who would be going to the Pacific. I was on that list and was quite disappointed because in my mind I was sure I would be shipped to Germany. It did not make sense to me. I would have been so much more valuable to the army in Germany. I also had a stronger incentive to fight the Germans. I talked to one of my officers, explaining my feelings, but he could only sympathize with me and state, "That's the army for you!" Soon we were on our way to Camp Adare at Vancouver Barracks in the Washington State to be processed for our voyage to the Pacific. Though at Vancouver only briefly, we did have one free Sunday when a friend and I decided to hitchhike to Salem, Oregon, about 60 miles south of our camp and supposedly not as congested with GIs as was Portland just across the river, which we had visited twice before.

We reached Salem around 11 A.M., and as we wandered aimlessly, an elderly couple started to engage us in conversation. They had just come from church services and had a son of their own in the service. They invited us to their home for Sunday dinner, and having no better plans, we accepted. They introduced themselves as Doctor and Mrs. H. Winiecki. They told us that they frequently took in GIs who looked a little lonely. They treated us to a wonderful home-cooked dinner and then entertained us with pleasant conversation, music, games of horseshoes, and a few games of chess. We left to return to base late in the afternoon. Their warm hospitality to complete strangers left a deep impression on me. I corresponded with them for a number of years. What a wonderfully friendly and patriotic gesture! It reflected the mood of the country at its best during the war.

At Vancouver Barracks, we exchanged our old military clothing for new clothing suitable for the tropics. We received a battery of vaccinations and physical exams and then packed our gear and boarded a troop transport, the U.S.S. *Bolivar*—APA 34, docked at Vancouver, Washington, on the Columbia River.

Chapter 14

Overseas

The U.S.S. *Bolivar* was no luxury liner. She was defined as an attack transport and had seen plenty of action. She delivered troops at Leyte on D-Day, the 20th of October 1944, and the same on D-Day at Lingayen, the 9th of January 1945, as well as on Iwo Jima on D+3, the 21st of February 1945, and now we were aboard. For armament there was a five-inch gun, a quad heavy caliber antiaircraft machine gun, and many — I recall counting twenty — twenty mm guns. After I saw the armaments, which were substantial for a troop ship, and heard a lecture on the ship's combat history, I became quite concerned that we too might be landed in an active combat area. I did not feel that we were ready for that. As replacement troops we were only loosely organized and had not trained as a unit. Oh God, don't let the army make another mistake!

We were packed like sardines, four bunks high. There were over one thousand of us aside from the crew. The quarters were hot and smelly, so we spent as much time as possible on deck. To pass the time, when we did not clean our rifles or stand inspection, we played poker, checkers, and chess. I still had the small portable chess set given to me by a friend before I left Germany. The game board was about six inches square, and each little chess piece had a small dowel at its base to fit into a hole in the board. As the ship left the dock to move down the Columbia River toward the Pacific Ocean, I was deeply involved in a lengthy game of chess. Suddenly I became nauseous. When I got to the ship's rail, I noticed that we had just passed the estuary of the Columbia River. We were feeling the first swells of the Pacific Ocean. From that moment I was seasick until we landed on the island of Leyte in the Philippines. The lengthy trip was worse for me than the Atlantic crossing five years earlier because there was little sympathy on this ship for my discomfort; at times I thought I would die, and at times I hoped I would die. I felt unbelievably nauseous and weak for the entire trip. I forced myself to eat a little and lost weight and strength, but in the end I survived. However, one of my little chess men did not make it. It fell overboard one day when I was trying to do both—play chess and vomit at the same time. As we approached our destination, we could see land masses on the horizon and to our sides; however, it was not until the day before we landed that we were officially told that we would land at Leyte, an island in the central Philippines. It had been liberated from the Japanese in October 1944, at which time General Douglas MacArthur had come ashore on precisely the same beach at which we landed in June 1945.

The docking facilities at Leyte were still very primitive, so we had to disembark by climbing down rope cargo nets slung over the side of the ship and into landing boats. As soon as each landing boat was filled, it took off for the short trip to shore, rammed onto the beach, and dropped its front gate so we could walk right off the boat and onto the beach. The beach we landed on was near the town of Tacloban. Within an hour of landing, my feeling of sea sickness was pretty well gone, but Leyte was stifling hot and drenchingly humid. Once ashore, while waiting for the others to disembark, we looked for a shady spot to rest and found clusters of coconut trees that offered some protection from the beastly sun. Within a short while we suffered our first casualty. One fellow near us had the misfortune of having a ripe coconut fall from the tree and hit him on the head, causing him to slump over unconscious. We were immediately ordered to put on our steel helmets.

In the afternoon we were transported to an improvised replacement camp from where we were assigned to whatever field unit needed men. I was to join an artillery unit on the island of Luzon. The fact that I was infantry, not artillery, did not seem to matter. This unit had the heaviest guns in the army, the 240 mm weapons. Transit to Luzon was by LST (landing ship tank), one of the most unseaworthy types of ships in the navy. Our LST was large but slow, and it took almost three days of travel in very uncomfortable accommodations before we reached our destination. Fortunately we traveled in calm waters, and I experienced little seasickness.

The Philippines consists of over 7000 islands of which Luzon is the largest, most populated, and strategically the most important. The Japanese hold outs were still fighting on Luzon mainly in and around the capital city of Manila. Our destination was the Lingayen Gulf north of Manila. This was where the American Sixth Army had landed in January 1945.

When we arrived at Lingayen, the port facilities were so heavily damaged that the heavy 240 mm guns could not be unloaded. They had been intended to destroy the last Japanese holdouts in the old walled city (Intramuros) in Manila. After a day or two, I was reassigned to the 518th AAA (anti-aircraft artillery) battalion. There were hardly any Japanese aircraft in the area, thanks to some very successful naval battles in the Leyte Gulf area in which several Japanese aircraft carriers were destroyed. Consequently, the 518th was reassigned to do the big guns' job—help destroy the last organized Japanese resistance in the Intramuros of Manila.

Our unit, Battery C, consisted of four 90 mm anti-aircraft guns, which although designed to shoot at aircraft could also be fired horizontally at ground targets. Not being familiar with this equipment, and having no seniority, I was assigned to an ammunition detail. This duty involved accompanying a 2 1/2-ton truck or a DUKW (an amphibious vehicle that can move on both land and water). We usually drove the vehicle empty from Manila to a depot near Lingayen, about 100 miles north of Manila. We loaded it with cases of 90 mm shells and then drove back to Manila to unload the ammunition near our guns. We did this once each day. We drove at breakneck speed so we would get more free time but also because Japanese snipers took frequent shots at us as we drove through the hinterland. We realized that just one unlucky shot could blow up the vehicle with all of us aboard, but we were lucky. Nothing happened to us.

I spent several weeks on ammunition detail before the shelling of the Intramuros took its toll. The Japanese soldiers had a military code, adapted from the ancient Samurai ethos of *Bushido*, which viewed surrender as the ultimate dishonor. Rather than give up, the holdouts fought to the death and soon were completely destroyed. After resistance ceased at the Intramuros, we returned to the battery's prior assignment of guarding the air space over Clark Field, about 60 miles north of Manila. Since fighting in the Philippines was essentially over, we all realized that the Japanese mainland would be the next major target. Would the Japanese surrender without an invasion of the mainland? We watched the news to see if air power alone could do the job.

While the Americans were beating the Japanese in the Philippines and Okinawa, the U.S. Air Corps was doing all the damage it could to the Japanese mainland. On March 9, 1945, 335 Superfortress bombers firebombed Tokyo, leaving 90,000 dead and about 1 million homeless. During the next six months, General LeMay, the commander of the U.S. Air Force Strategic

Air Command (SAC), ordered the bombing of sixty-six of Japan's largest cities. Excluded in this bombing were the cities of Hiroshima and Nagasaki. More than eight million people lost their homes and 900,000 were killed, and yet the Japanese spirit did not flex. Japan would fight to the last drop of blood. The only way to end the war would be to invade Japan. That prospect was terrible to contemplate in terms of lives that would be lost, both American and Japanese.

Shortly after relocating to Clark Field, I became an apprentice mechanic and was promoted to private first class. We started to receive preparatory training for our next assignment, the invasion of the Japanese mainland. A very scary thought indeed! The scuttlebutt was that there would be at least one million American casualties. That statistic was of major concerned all of us.

Then, on August 6, we heard that a super bomb, a nuclear bomb, more powerful than a thousand bombs, had been dropped on Japan. A few days later, another one. On August 14, 1945 Japan surrendered. The war was over!

We were ecstatic and relieved not to have to invade Japan. We were so overjoyed that we fired our 90 mm antiaircraft guns repeatedly. Shortly thereafter a terse message from headquarters arrived: "There will be no further indiscriminate shooting of firearms." The big guns stopped firing, but we just couldn't resist the temptation to celebrate, so we fired our carbines into the air for several more hours.[10]

When we lined up for evening chow, a Filipino kitchen worker called out in distress. He had seen some Japanese soldiers. Several Japanese soldiers who had been roaming in the nearby jungle had come to the perimeter of our location. Later we found out that

---

[10]Note: As an infantryman I had a M1 rifle, but when I was assigned to the artillery the personal weapon was a carbine, which is a lighter weapon that fires the same ammunition but with less power and less accuracy.

they wanted to investigate the shooting, thinking they might rejoin fellow soldiers whom they believed we were shooting at. Over a portable P.A. system, a Japanese-speaking Filipino attached to our unit haltingly explained to them that the war was over and there would be no disgrace in coming forward (surrendering), and that would get them back to Japan.

Before long, several Japanese soldiers, starved and disheveled, hesitantly raised a white rag to indicate their surrender. Relieved of their weapons, they were taken prisoner and offered food. Over the next week or so more than twenty Japanese stragglers surrendered to our unit. It was one of the largest groups of Japanese soldiers to surrender during the entire Philippines campaign. Their Bushido creed is what kept most others from surrendering. To snag the stragglers who were ready to surrender, we posted armed guards at our chow lines to receive them when they came within sight. The first soldiers to surrender were a great curiosity to me. They were smaller and much less intimidating than I had envisioned. They were of course scared but very humble, bowing at almost everybody. I wondered if they expected the cruel treatment they dished out to American prisoners during the Death March after Corregidor fell to them in 1942. That was certainly not the treatment they got from us. The first thing we did for them after checking them for weapons was to give them food and water. Then, they were allowed to wash, after which they were put in one of our tents. Of course they were under guard at all times, but no one touched them or verbally abused them. Later, MPs (military police) came and took them away. This procedure was followed each day we had surrenders.

Our unit received a citation for capturing them even though the war was over, and we really made little attempt to do the capturing. This was but one of the idiosyncrasies of my military career.

Now that the war had ended, we tried to make life a little more comfortable for ourselves. Our battery had hired some

Filipinos to do the kitchen chores, and that meant no more K.P. To reduce our personal chores, an ample supply of "laundry girls" offered to do our laundry, make our beds, and do almost anything we asked of them for some food, some soap, and an occasional dollar for exceptional service. My laundry girl's name was Mary. She was at most 16 years old and was amazingly obliging. I think she hoped that I might take her back to America with me. I believe most of the laundry girls lived with such illusions. Mary had several smaller brothers who tried desperately to ingratiate themselves with me by continually offering to help me even when I needed absolutely no help. Once when I visited Mary's home I saw that the pride of the family home was a foot-operated antique Singer sewing machine. I believe that qualified Mary's mother as the village seamstress or at least as one of the village seamstresses. I was interested in their lifestyle but did not want to get involved or be misunderstood, and so kept my contact with her family to a minimum.

The Filipinos all came from a very small village nearby where the houses consisted of one or two rooms on stilts; their water buffaloes and chickens were quartered in the space below the living quarters. The village had no electricity and no running water. Our encampment looked luxurious by comparison. We had improvised showers and had ample water from a water truck, but we lacked proper toilets. One evening, our first sergeant and a group of about twenty of us "volunteers" took two of our trucks on an unofficial mission to nearby Clark Field. We loaded a huge empty wooden crate, about 8 feet by 8 feet by 16 feet onto one truck while we rode on the other, and returned to our encampment. With a little ingenuity we converted the crate into a multiple seat toilet, with electric light and covers for the toilet holes. This minimized the odor from the pit below.

Life was routine, but it was bearable. Malaria was a constant threat. We took Adaprine pills daily to keep the malediction at bay. The worst problem was boredom and the realization that we were wasting our lives away for no good purpose. I wanted to get on with my life by learning a profession and be able to do something useful. With the war over, this desultory lifestyle was not my idea of living.

Chapter 15

Coming Home

Once peace was established, troops who had been overseas and fighting for years were extremely anxious to get back home. To figure out who should have priority, the Army created a point system: one point for each month in the service, a second point for each month overseas, five points for each combat campaign and additional points for medals. After having accumulated seventy-five points, a soldier was entitled to be sent home. Some of the men in our unit had been in service for over three years and had a great many points. I had less than twenty. To reduce the pressure of entitled GIs demanding to go home, and to avoid the disintegration of army units, the Army announced a special program: If a soldier stationed overseas reenlisted for one year in the regular Army[11], he would get a four-week furlough and a choice of "theater of operation," or country in which to serve the year. There was much discussion among the men regarding the pros and cons of this program.

---

[11]Draftees were technically in a different Army than the official "regular Army."

Generally, those with seventy-five points who were entitled to go home did not enlist for another year. I felt that if I waited my turn, I might be stuck in the Philippines for almost that long, whereas if I reenlisted, I could plan my future and select the United States as my theater of operations.

On November 26, 1945, I signed the reenlistment papers. This was about one week after the Army made the offer. The following week, the program was stopped because it was not achieving its objective. Generally, those who had been overseas for a short time signed up, while the experienced old timers for whom the program was intended did not. However, I was in the program before it closed, so I was in line to go back to the States before the end of 1945.

While awaiting my transfer, I heard through letters from home that Uncle Mor, who had enlisted as a doctor in 1942 and served in France, Belgium, and Germany, was now in the Philippines. In an effort to locate him, I went to the main military post office to find out where his unit, the 231st General Hospital Unit, was located. When I finally did make contact, his group was in the process of being shipped to Japan. However, we did meet for an hour or so. It was great exchanging news of the family. I felt very proud that he now looked at me as a man rather than the boy whom he cared for not so long ago. It is of interest that Uncle Mor was one of the few men who served in the German Army in World War I and in the U.S. Army in World War II.

With more leisure time, my companions and I frequently visited Manila, which, although thoroughly destroyed, was rapidly reestablishing itself as the place where the action was. To get to Manila fast, we would go to Clark Field to hitch a ride in a cargo plane, but we had to be willing to sit in the cargo hatch and absorb the bouncing that the pilots seemed to enjoy adding to the already un-cushioned ride.

In November, there was a notice to reenlisters that if they volunteered to help modify a Liberty ship (cargo ship) for use as a troop transport, they would be assured a berth on it. I and several others decided to accept the offer based on the concept that "a bird in the hand is worth two in the bush." We were consequently transferred to Manila for two weeks and helped bolt the wooden two-by-fours in place to hold the canvas cots that would serve as our beds. In early December, we boarded and left the Philippines. After a week on the ocean, our ship's propulsion system broke down. We floated on the ocean like a cork. I was seasick before the ship failed, and only got worse once we stopped moving and just bobbed up and down. This homeward bound trip was worse than the two previous ocean crossings, but the anticipation of being home again softened the pain.

A day or two after the breakdown, a seagoing tugboat came and towed our ship into Pearl Harbor, Hawaii. We were there for about a week, quartered in pup tents at Hickham Field. There was plenty of free time for us, and we decided to visit the famous Royal Hawaiian Hotel and Waikiki Beach. When we arrived there, the hotel was off limits to enlisted men and the beach was a bit of a disappointment as it was only a few feet wide. Beyond that we really didn't know our way around. We were therefore happy to hear that we would soon board another vessel for the remainder of the trip home. I had by now become a bit more savvy, and once at sea again, instead of lining up for chow along the ship's engine room with its inherent oil exhaust odor, which aggravated my persistent nausea, I now got some of my buddies to fetch me an apple or some toast and bring it to me topside. I was still not a sailor, but I had learned to minimize my seasickness.

We docked in California, and disembarked at Camp Ross on December 26, 1945. I was ecstatic that the sea and seasickness were behind me. On December 28, several of us received vouchers for a flight to New York on TWA. The flight consisted of several hops in a DC 3 aircraft, a propeller plane which had a relatively short range and therefore stopped several times for refueling. I did not arrive in New York until January 1, 1946. While in flight, we kidded each other that this was the "highest" we'd ever get on New Year's Eve.

From New York we were bussed to Fort Dix, New Jersey, were we were supplied with new uniforms, and I received my thirty-day furlough. I boarded the bus to Manhattan. When I rang the doorbell on January 3, 1946 I was warmly embraced by Mom and Inge. We talked late into the evening, catching up on all the events that had taken place since we last parted company.

The worst news was of the situation of Jews in Germany, specifically my grandmother, uncle, aunt, and cousin. It was only after the defeat of Germany that the unbelievable truths were confirmed. Of the almost seven million Jews in Europe at the start of the war, only about 500,000 survived. All the others were dead: shot, gassed, burned, starved, killed or dead in some other horrible way. They were destroyed in unbelievably cruel ways because so many Germans, Poles and others lost all concepts of humanity. They treated the Jews worse than any animal for no reason other than that they were Jews. Terrible, almost unbelievable stories started to permeate the German Jewish communities in America in the form of rumors and unconfirmed reports. Then the first confirmation of catastrophic events arrived from military reports from troops who, in the course of their advance liberated the concentration camps. News reporters who followed up on these reports, not only reconfirmed the cruel events at the concentration camps but uncovered the broader aspects of the Holocaust. Soon thereafter, survivors from the concentration camps and others, "displaced persons," people who had lost everything and had no place to go, bore further witness to the truth of the inhumanity. One such witness was Gisela Eckstein, the second cousin of mine with whom I played as a child in Battenberg. She and her family, mother, father and brother were sent to concentration camps. All of her family was exterminated except for her. She survived, although permanently damaged, both mentally and physically. After some time in a displaced persons camp, she managed to get to America where she told us of her tormented experiences. Mother had gotten some confirmation of the fate of our family through the Red Cross and some from other survivors who at various times had contact with them. As for our immediate family members left in Germany, my grandmother had become ill, could not get medical help and died. My cousin Gerd somehow got to Switzerland where he stayed briefly, but the Swiss authorities forced him to leave. He got onto a ship bound for England. The ship was torpedoed and Gerd drowned. When his father, Uncle Walter, learned of Gerd's death, his despondency added to the destitution, hopelessness, and increasing Nazi persecution led him to commit suicide by hanging. His wife, Aunt Klara, his brother-in-law, and Klara's parents were rounded up and they died in one of Hitler's concentration camps. None of my mother's efforts to locate them or get further details of their demise were successful. She was informed that all that was known was that they had succumbed to Hitler's "Final Solution" of the Jews. Thus, our entire family on my mother's side vanished in the Holocaust.

That first night at home as I tried to go to sleep, all of this news, which I had not focused on previously, kept stirring in my mind. My mind was filled with contrasting emotions — anger at the perpetrators, sympathy for the victims and a feeling of guilt because I survived in relative comfort while they suffered and died. Despite the joy of my homecoming, the specter of the Holocaust in Europe did not leave me alone. How could God have permitted such cruelty and suffering, especially when it came to innocent children? But then I thought of the insignificance of our world in the vastness and the complexity of the universe. I thought of such diverse godly creations as the structure of atoms, the infinity of space, the miracles of nature such as birth. I thought of all the things I do not understand and this brought me to the conclusion that God cannot be just a superior image of man. What we call God must be our word for something our feeble human mind just can not comprehend. And thus we try to live in accordance with the best rules developed by inspired men and accept what fate delivers to us. In that light our traditions are the glue that holds us together.

Life does go on. The day following my homecoming, Inge and Mother went to work. I slept late and tried to relax and lay the demons of my mind to rest. The next day, Saturday, Mother could not repress her urge to show off her soldier boy, tanned and healthy looking from the tropical sun. First, we visited Aunt Bina of whom I was very fond. She was my mother's cousin who came to visit us in Battenberg after my father died to give solace, and who was supportive when we were in Frankfurt. Next we paid a visit to my mother's friend, Lina Marx, the widow of my father's cousin and the mother of Manfred, who met me at the pier when I arrived in America from England. As we left Lina's apartment, Mother suggested we stop for a moment at the Greenebaums who lived in the same building. The Greenebaums had recently become friends of my mother through Frieda Greenebaum, who owned a beauty parlor and was Inge's employer and friend.

The Greenebaum family consisted of Frieda, her husband Eric, her parents, Thekla and Isaac and her daughter, Susan. Susan was then about two years old, a beautiful child, but with an apparent serious disability. She did not behave right and uttered only strange sounds.

While Inge worked at the beauty parlor, Frida's 18-year-old cousin Henrietta Alexander occasionally visited and sometimes came in to help as well as enjoy the gossip and camaraderie of the women at the beauty parlor. Inge mentioned in conversation that she had a brother in the army and suggested to Henrietta that she should write to him. But Henrietta, whom everyone called Henny, voiced the opinion that by the standards of the time, he should make the first move and write to her. While I was overseas, Inge mentioned this conversation in correspondence to me. I did not take her up on it, and it pretty much left my thoughts.

So, back to our imminent visit to the Greenebaums. Mother rang the doorbell of the apartment, and Thekla warmly beckoned us to enter. As I surveyed the living room, I noticed a very attractive young lady sitting on the floor, playing with the little child. She rose as Thekla introduced her: "This is Henny." I felt strange pangs throughout my entire bodily system. Instantly my sister's letter reentered my consciousness. This young lady was beautiful. To me she looked like the All American girl. A smooth complexion, a pageboy hairstyle, white freshly starched blouse and Scottish plaid skirt, white socks and pristine saddle leather shoes, petite build but of very pleasant proportions. I felt instantly infatuated and with some difficulty tried to make small talk. I noticed a bit of timidity on her part, which only enhanced the impression she made. As we talked, my bashfulness disintegrated and before our visit came to an end, I was so smitten that I asked Henny for a date to meet again that evening. To my delight, she accepted.

The rest of that day I felt great—until suppertime when friends and neighbors inundated our apartment, wishing to welcome me home. What a terrible predicament! I had a date with Henny and a house full of well-wishers, and more were arriving. In desperation I called Henny and explained. As we conversed, I was overwhelmed to discover an admirable trait in her—compassion. Perhaps I did sense a bit of disappointment in her voice. That only served to assure me to press for reestablishing our date the following day, Sunday the sixth of January—without fail.

And so Henny and I had our first date. I met her at her apartment at 3036 Bailey Avenue in the West Bronx. We took the subway downtown and saw the movie *The Lost Weekend* starring Ray Millard in the Rivoli Theater. We had a great time together, finding ourselves very compatible. Henny was in her first year at Hunter College. I was planning to go to college after I was discharged from the Army which would be by the end of 1946. Henny was Jewish but not very observant in regard to ritual and *kashrith*, and neither was I. We both came from Germany, but Henny's English pronunciation was flawless, unlike mine.

Henny was born in the village of Rehlingen in the Saar district. The Saar was part of Germany until after World War I, when France, anxious to reap the economic benefits from the Saar's rich coal resources, requested that the Saar be placed under French administration for fifteen years or until 1935. At that time the people of the Saar would vote to determine whether they wanted to remain part of France or return to German jurisdiction. This plan was incorporated in the Versailles Peace Treaty.

By 1935, however, Hitler was in power, and he rigged the vote so that the outcome would favor Germany. He offered free transportation plus a bonus to any German who could make any claim to have lived or whose ancestors had lived in the Saar. He then sent agents into the Saar to organize and where necessary intimidate the natives to vote for German reunification. The result was return of the Saar to Germany. As part of the agreement, any resident of the Saar who so wanted could leave during a limited window of opportunity. As soon as the Saar was back under German administration, Nazi anti-Semitism manifested itself.

Henny's father, Max, had a butcher shop and employed a non-Jewish apprentice Alvis Kraemer. Max tried to keep the business going, but within a year he realized that there was no future for his family in Germany. He sold his house and business and moved to nearby Luxembourg, which he viewed as a temporary haven. When he sold his house and business, however, that transaction was under duress. Alvis threatened him at the point of a gun stating that he, Alvis, would get the business or no one would. So Alvis got the house and business pretty much at his own price.

Because Luxembourg was suffering from widespread unemployment, foreigners were not allowed to work. Max, his wife, Lilly, and his three children, Marcel, Edith and Henny, thus lived there on the family's transferred savings for about a year until Max's brother Siegfried was able to help them emigrate to the United States, which they did in 1937.

Chapter 16

My Last Year in the Army

During my January furlough, Henny attended Hunter College on weekdays, and on weekends we enjoyed time together. I was to report to Fort Hancock, New Jersey on February 3, 1946. I had been assigned there for two weeks, after which I would be transferred to Fort Bliss, Texas, my permanent station for the balance of my army enlistment. During those two weeks, I went home to visit for two weekends. Of course, I spent a good part of each weekend in Henny's company. On one of these weekends, when I arrived at Henny's home, there were visitors who also had immigrated from Rehlingen, the Gunther family. I met their son, Edgar, who was in uniform. He was a sergeant in the Military Intelligence. In conversation, he asked whether I would not rather be stationed in his group in Camp Ritchie, Maryland. I said, "Of course, but you know that my military assignment is beyond my control." He claimed to be able to request my transfer and wrote down my forthcoming military address at Fort Bliss. I had absolutely no faith in his braggadocio claims, but to be polite, I just said I would look forward to the transfer.

I felt very depressed not to enjoy Henny's company once I went to Texas, but we had promised to write to each other, which we did. I reported for duty at Fort Bliss on February 18, 1946, and was enrolled in a course on antiaircraft weapons mechanics. I had previously been an antiaircraft artillery mechanic's assistant but had never had formal training in that specialty, so the course was an excellent supplement to my practical experience.

My prior experience, as well as my aptitude made me number one in the graduating class of the six-week course. Hence, and because of my knowledge of German, I was selected for a team whose mission it was to evaluate captured German 88 mm guns. These were reputed to be the best of their kind and superior to the 90 mm guns used by the U.S. Army.

Each day our team drove about 80 miles to the White Sands Proving Grounds in New Mexico, towing a German 88 mm antiaircraft gun. We then prepared it for firing. An aircraft would tow a target sleeve that we were to shoot at while recording the gun settings such as charge, fuse type, deflection, elevation, and sight inclination. We soon became so adept at firing and the weapon was so accurate that we aimed for the precise spot where the target sleeve joined the tow line. This would sever the target, and we would have one or more hour's rest while the plane landed to get a new target sleeve.

Our weekend recreation consisted primarily of going to the bull fights in Juarez, Mexico, just across the border. The bridge across the Rio Grande River was a toll bridge. The toll was two cents U.S. currency; for most Mexicans this cost was sufficient to prevent their frequent crossing. At the bull fights, we GIs sat on the shady side of the ring which was more expensive—50 cents is my recollection—rather than on the sunny side of the ring, which was cheaper. The Mexicans cheered for the toreador, but the GIs generally cheered for the bull. When the show was over, there were menacing glances from the stimulated Mexicans and some incomprehensible outcries, but nothing serious happened. I believe the Mexicans realized that they were at a physical disadvantage since we GIs were in prime physical shape and even in the mood for a little action, especially after we were fortified by copious quantities of beer consumed before and during the bull fights.

I had been at Fort Bliss about two months when I was summoned to the office of Colonel Von Volkenburg, the head man at the Fort. I was very nervous and could not imagine which of my careless acts brought me to this reckoning. What had I done that was so bad that I would be called to the "holy cow?" Perhaps our shooting at the target tow line joints instead of the center of the target? Perhaps something we did in Mexico? I was exceedingly apprehensive, much as one is when a policeman signals to pull over when cruising along on the highway at a slightly excessive speed.

I saluted sharply as I was ushered into his office and stood at attention. He voiced the standard command, "At ease," and I relaxed only slightly. Then he asked if I knew why I was called. I cautiously stated that I did not know. He then asked me to sit down and proceeded to fire a battery of questions regarding my past military experience, emphasizing the subject of security: How I handled security at Fort Bliss and what I thought of security at Fort Bliss and White Sands. I was flabbergasted that the top man at this post would ask such questions of a lowly soldier. Why was he asking them? What security regulation had I violated? I was fearful of some kind of trap. He seemed especially interested in why I had reenlisted. (from a draftee to a member of the regular Army). I tried to fit my answers to what I thought he might want to hear, within the limits of the truth. I was totally confused by the emphasis on security and the attention I was getting. I felt like a mouse being played with by a cat. Finally, he told me that he had received a request from the "top" for my transfer to the Military Intelligence Center at Camp Ritchie. My orders were to travel alone, and that Major Bowman, the camp's Executive officer, would attend to my transfer papers and my transit to the El Paso railroad station. It was now my impression that the colonel thought I might be an army counterintelligence agent checking up on security matters at the fort. Of course, he never said that, but I was still unsure what it was all about until the realization hit me that this was the transfer that Henny's acquaintance—I had forgotten his name—had said he could arrange.

I arrived at Camp Ritchie on April 7. Camp Ritchie was the prime venue for training military intelligence personnel and was the repository of most of the documents captured from the German Army. A select group of German prisoners of war were also housed there to assist in the organization and utilization of these documents. These POWs were under the supervision of the U.S. Army's German Military Document Section, known as GMDS. Most of the members of this section were former German Jewish immigrants.

By now I fully realized with a mixture of chagrin and satisfaction that Edgar Gunther's claim to be able to have me transferred was for real. Here I was, just a few hours away from home and Henny. I reported in at headquarters of GMDS, and a sergeant, Fritz Mandell, cordially welcomed me. Aside from the official transfer notice, Edgar Gunther had alerted him to my coming. Once signed in, Fritz suggested that as soon as I was settled in my assigned quarters I should go to barrack "A" where I should ask for Sergeant Schmitt. He would show me around. The cordiality and informality of this initial contact hardly seemed like the U.S. Army.

As I entered barrack "A," I saw nothing but German prisoners of war, all energetically packing bundles of documents. This was my first exposure to German war prisoners. The sight of these men in fatigue uniforms with "PW" stenciled on them in large letters startled me. Unlike the Japanese prisoners I had recently encountered, most of these men were tall, looked well fed and appeared to be of cheerful disposition. In this first impression, I observed no humility or inhibition. To my surprise, I saw no American guards. There were none, just German POWs. Awkwardly trying to manifest some authority, in as firm a voice as I could muster, I asked to no one in particular, "Sergeant Schmitt?"

Immediately, one of the men nearby me shouted, *"Feldwebel Schmitt, kommen sie hier"* (come here). In an instant, a small heavyset man came forward and introduced himself as Schmitt. He spoke reasonably good English and with a smiling demeanor told me he was expecting me and was pleased to meet me. I was surprised at his apparent cordiality. After all, this was the enemy. What crimes against humanity might he have committed? Did he know that I was Jewish? He gave me a VIP tour, explaining that he was one of a group of volunteer prisoners of war who had helped to organize the captured German documents that were about to be shipped to the Pentagon. The volunteers were presently bundling the documents and labeling the bundles. After the documents were shipped out, the POWs would return to Germany. They were one of the last contingents of German Prisoners of war still in the United States.

Continuing the discourse, he stated, "Of course we are anxious to get back home, but we were not Hitler supporters, and the war was a big mistake."

I wondered if I should believe him and thought to test his authenticity. I said, "You know, I am Jewish and got kicked out of Germany because of that."

Without hesitation he answered, "Almost all the Americans I have worked with here at Camp Ritchie are former German Jews, and they are really great guys. Having spent time here has made me and my fellow workers realize how wrong Hitler was with his anti-Semitism. I can only say I am sorry, and that this cataclysm should never have happened. The Germans are really not bad people." I could not agree but let it go at that and let him complete the tour without much further conversation.

That evening, Ed Gunther welcomed me, and we attended a little welcoming party he'd arranged to introduce me to the rest of the GMDS members. Also at the party were several British and Canadian soldiers. The captured German documents that included the entire German Armed Forces Archives, which were jointly "owned" by the British, Canadians, and Americans, and these men were here to help exploit this treasure chest of intelligence. Over the next few days I watched as the thousands of bundles, each about a cubic foot in size, were meticulously loaded into huge military vans. The bundles were labeled and loaded in a prearranged sequence. If a bundle fell or was out of order, the loading was stopped until the sequence was correctly reestablished. I watched German precision in full force. However, what did sent goose bumps down my spine and irritation through my system was when I heard them in unison singing German songs in marching cadence as they did their work of loading. Memories are easily stirred up!

By April 16, all documents were loaded. The German POWs boarded busses to the ship that would take them home, while our unit received the anticipated orders to transfer to South Post of Fort Myers, Virginia, which was a small encampment next to the Pentagon. I was the newest member of the GMDS, which consisted of almost a dozen officers and seventeen enlisted men of various ranks. Also attached to our unit were the Canadian and British army associates. I was the only private first class (PFC). There were two corporals, Tom Kline and Joe Brennan. The remaining noncommissioned officers were sergeants of various ranks, including of course Ed Gunther.

The first task at our new location was going to be re-shelving the documents, which had preceded our convoy in a fleet of huge vans. We arrived at the large unloading area in the Pentagon where we found the documents piled helter-skelter in a tremendous pyramid, with many of the cords used to tie the bundles broken. Apparently, since there was no manpower to unload the cargo carefully, the van drivers had used a dump-

and-run method of unloading, which had the effect of undoing completely the careful loading effort of the German POWs back at Camp Ritchie.

It took us about three months to make some sense of the pile of papers. We never fully straightened out the mess while I was there.

As soon as we had some of the documents organized, we received requests for documents from a large variety of interests, among them staff lawyers for the Nuremberg trials. These were trials by an international court, the first of its kind, to bring to justice German leaders who committed crimes against humanity by being responsible for the deaths of many, many millions of innocent people. Many documents in our care were valuable as evidence. We helped the researchers as much as we could. It is quite possible that our effort resulted in the conviction of some of Hitler's henchmen. That was very satisfying to me.

As we continued putting the documents back in order, demands for translations arrived. I was assigned to a task force that worked with the U.S. military historic branch to assemble German documentation of the Anzio Beachhead in Italy. The team correlated these with equivalent U.S. army documentation. Some startling observations emerged. Here is one small but typical example: a German report stated that they were unable to repair three of their tanks which were unusable because of generator failure while a corresponding American patrol report stated that three German tanks were sighted and they seemed to be being prepared for attack. Generally, our work highlighted the inaccuracy of patrol reports on both sides, and showed how actions based on these reports led to the failures and losses in battle. It also revealed that by sheer superiority of troop numbers and equipment, the U.S. survived and in the end secured the beachhead. The report was mimeographed on cheap paper; a copy which I kept disintegrated years later because of the brittleness of the paper.

Whenever we weren't translating or filling document loan requests, we continued the never-ending chore of trying to file the documents that were disorganized in the transit from Camp Ritchie. On top of that, more cases of documents continued to arrive from Germany. We received several cases of magnetic wire recordings from German camps for Allied prisoners called *Stalags*. These recordings of the prisoners' quarters were made without the prisoners' knowledge. We also received German wire recorder/playback units so that we could listen to the recordings. Unfortunately these machines had poor fidelity and no fast-forward feature. Our job was to catalog their contents. At first, this task seemed interesting, but after a while it became thoroughly boring. Between bits of interesting conversations, there were hours of small talk. Most of the conversations were unintelligible. After several weeks we finally gave up and had the recordings shipped to an army warehouse in Virginia.

Although the GMDS occupied a huge part of the mezzanine basement of one fifth of the Pentagon, this space was not large enough to hold the massive quantity of documents on hand. (Remember that the Pentagon was probably the largest building in the country in terms of office space.) In an effort to gain some space, one of our officers requested permission to dispose of certain personnel files of German officers. Each officer, and there were over a million of these, had a personnel file (called a 201 file) containing, among other things, his commission, behavior reports, promotions and discharge orders. Additionally, we had a huge series of files containing the same orders, filed in chronological sequence. We asked whether we could get rid of the chronological files since data requests were almost always by name of officer. Our request was approved providing we photocopied each document to be destroyed. So much for military intelligence logic. We ended up ignoring the response and getting rid of most of the duplicate documents. A few were kept as souvenirs. Ed Gunther had the entire set of promotion orders of General Rommel. I had a few random ones that I kept for their seals and the signatures. The signatories included Nazi leaders such as Hitler, Keitel, Guderian, and Blomberg as well as the old German President Hindenburg.

Work at GMDS was much like working in any office. We worked from 8 A.M. to 5 P.M. and closed early on Fridays. That enabled us to visit our families or nearby relatives on weekends. About once a month I traveled to New York, either by hitchhiking or train, depending on my finances, the weather, and time. Hitchhiking for GIs was very much encouraged by the government and well supported by the public at large. When I hitchhiked, I took the streetcars to the northeastern limit of D.C. and then thumbed rides to Newark or New York City, where I again took local transit home. I generally arrived home late Friday evening, had a pleasurable date with Henny on Saturday, and left for Washington late Sunday. If I did not go to New York, I might visit the Simons in Baltimore or the Stahls in Vineland. Sometimes I just stayed in Washington.

I became quite friendly with a coworker, Tom Kline, and we sometimes toured Washington to see the sights of our capital. Tom was born in the Sudeten part of Czechoslovakia and escaped with his family to Ecuador when the Germans forcibly acquired the Sudeten part of Czechoslovakia in 1938. Tom obtained a job with an American official stationed in Ecuador, and that official aided him in coming to this country. Immediately upon his arrival here, he was drafted into the Army. Tom, not having any other exposure to the United States, planned to stay in the service. He later reenlisted and worked his way up to the ranks of colonel. When we were at GMDS, he was one rank ahead of me, but that never affected our friendship then or now.

When I came to GMDS, I held the rank of private first class. That meant I had one chevron on my sleeve. However, the "table of organization" for GMDS called for higher ranking noncommissioned officers, and some of the old timers were due for discharge from the Army so I had the good fortune to be promoted in rank as quickly as permissible by army regulations. I thus received a promotion almost every month. In June, 1946, I advanced to corporal (two chevrons), in July to buck sergeant (three chevrons), in August to staff sergeant (an inverted arch below the three chevrons), and in September to my final rank of tech sergeant (three chevrons and two inverted arches). While we worked at the Pentagon, administratively we were members of the prestigious Headquarters Company, War Department. This company included not only GMDS but also PACMIR (Pacific Military Intelligence Region), made up primarily of Nisei, Americans of Japanese descent. The Headquarters Company also included the honor guards who stood watch over the Tomb of the Unknown Soldier at the nearby Arlington Cemetery.

On one occasion, there was an order to rehearse marching, in anticipation of our possible participation in a parade in Washington. The honor guard had no problem performing as requested, but we members of GMDS and PACMIR performed so poorly that we were never asked to participate again.

On September 15, 1946, I came to New York to attend a party, celebrating my sister's engagement. She was happily betrothed to Lothar Braunschweiger. Lothar had recently been discharged from the army after having seen much combat in Europe including D-Day. He was now beginning his chosen career as a carpenter. When I heard that he was earning four dollars per hour, my reaction was that such pay was excessive, to say the least. No worker could be sufficiently productive to be worth that much. Even as a tech sergeant I only earned about $60 per month. Of course, as a GI, I did receive some indirect financial benefits. For example: Broadway theater tickets that regularly were $2.50 to $5.00 per seat were only 95 cents for soldiers. Train fare to Washington, D.C. for soldiers was about $4, and movie houses throughout the country offered substantial discounts to service men. As America shifted to a peacetime economy, these benefits slowly disappeared.

My time in Washington passed quickly, and on November 24, 1946, I was relieved of active duty. On December 1, I was officially discharged from the U.S. Army. I received my "ruptured duck" pin, a lapel pin given to each wartime soldier at the time of discharge. And so I was thrust into the world to start a new life.

Washington, D.C., 1946
Right to left: Fellow GMDS men, Matlow, Kline,
Thieburger. I am in squat position.

Washington, D.C., 1946
Me at my desk in the Pentagon.

Henny and Werner, engaged, 1949

Epilogue

Little by little I adapted to civilian life. I applied to City College of New York as an engineering undergraduate. Classes would start in February 1947. Under the GI Bill I received cost of tuition and a small allowance for food and lodging. I also obtained a part-time job at a startup company, Miles Reproducer Co., which produced sound recorders using steel needles and plastic film. I worked as a general helper, being placed wherever help was needed. I kept this job while in college and thus was able to save a little money after meeting my expenses and giving Mama a little support for the household. This job was fine while I attended college, but I recognized that the technology was outdated and watched as the company slowly succumbed to the technology of magnetic tape recorders. On nice days I often walked to college, a distance of about 35 blocks (from 173 Street to 137 Street), saving me the trolley fare of 5 cents each way. Weekends were almost always spent on dates with Henny.

Henny and I continued our ongoing relationship until spring of 1949 at which time Inge gave birth to her first child, Linda. We visited Inge at the hospital, and being very much stimulated by the event of a new baby in the family we decided to consider ourselves engaged. In June 1949 we attended Henny's Senior Prom, which sort of doubled as an engagement party. I had previously gone with Henny to a jeweler where we selected an engagement ring that cost more than anything I had ever bought before but I felt strongly that Henny was more than worth it. That year Henny graduated from Hunter College and obtained a job at Sky Top, a private kindergarten. She intended to keep this job only until she received her City Teaching Certificate. Private schools paid much less than public schools, so an appointment in a public school was her goal.

I had finished my first semester of college with a B average and then enrolled in summer school in the hope of finishing college in three and one-half years. I succeeded in doing just that, and in June 1950, I graduated. At that time national demobilization was at a peak. The armed services had released about fifteen million men to private industry while demand for labor was low. Millions of discharged servicemen had entered college under the GI Bill and had completed their studies at the same time I did. Jobs for beginning engineers were hard to find. In the absence of any more promising job, I grabbed at an offer as a model maker at a small company, Lester Associates. I thought this might be a way to earn some money and claim a little experience while I would continue to look for a "real" job in mechanical engineering. I was offered $40 per week, which was more than their entry level salary of $35 per week because I had a college degree.

Just as Henny and I settled into jobs, the world again shook as the United States, with the support of the United Nations, became embroiled in the Korean War. Communist North Korea had invaded noncommunist South Korea, and the U.S. was trying to save the noncommunist entity. America abruptly reversed its engines of industry to again produce armaments to fight another war.

With Henny and I both working and getting along splendidly, the obstacle to getting married was finding an apartment to live in. There was a severe shortage of apartments because there was no construction of apartments during the war, and many new families were forming. With the help of Henny's brother, we did obtain a reasonable place to live and thus we set our wedding date for Monday, December 25, 1950.

Our wedding was a formal affair. Henny wore a white satin princess-style gown with train. Lace framed the collar. Tiny buttons graced the front. She looked beautiful. I wore a gray vest, morning coat with tails, striped pants, ascot tie, and top hat. We decided on ten ushers, each wearing a tuxedo, top hat, and carrying a cane. They lined the aisle, and as we walked past, they raised their canes in salute so as to form a canopy, much like a military wedding with honor guards raising their swords. We shared the traditional wine and exchanged rings as part of our vows. I broke the traditional glass in memory of the destruction of the temple in Jerusalem and the suffering of the Jewish people. At that moment thoughts of Germany, of my father's death, of Kristall Nacht and of my mother's family destroyed by the Nazis once more ran fleetingly but hauntingly through my mind.

When I told my boss, Ray Lester, of my new status, he gave me a $4 per week raise to $44. At about the same time, the company received a major new contract for a large-scale detailed model of a Naval Destroyer Engine Room. Someone was needed who could read blueprints of the actual ship, the U.S.S. *Fletcher* (DD445). We would then be required to sketch out and draft the model parts to scale. This was easy for me with my engineering training, so I was assigned that work. In effect, with this task I started the Engineering Department of Lester Associates. Now my job looked a bit more promising than I had initially thought.

Henny received her New York City Teaching Certification and switched to a better-paying position.

Our new life together was quite harmonious, and by the end of our second year of marriage, Henny was pregnant, expecting our first child in early April, 1953. When I first saw my newborn son, he was held by a nurse who opened the blanket in which he was swaddled to permit me to see him fully. He still had spots of birth blood on his face and body. He had a substantial shock of black hair and seemed not to have a wrinkle on his body. My heart pulsed with excitement. It seemed miraculous that this little life was the product of our love. What a most wonderful feeling.

David had his *bris* and *pidion haben*: the first, a circumcision ritual to include him in the brotherhood of Abraham, making him officially Jewish; the second, a ritual of redeeming our first-born son by a token payment to a *Cohen* (priest).

We now had to learn to manage on my salary alone. By this time, my take-home pay had increased to $77 per week. Our work at Lester Associates had expanded to include contracts with the United Nations to make models of the new site on the East River in New York, and with IBM and Remington Rand Corp. to make models of their new product, computers. Every one of these early computers consisted of a number of components each bigger than a large refrigerator. A very sizable room was required to contain them. Models were thus helpful to show prospective customers what a computer would look like when installed. We built models of IBM's systems 702 and 705 and Remington Rand's Univac.

David grew nicely and made us very happy except for one thing. He had a stomach problem. He regurgitated milk curds after every bottle. Henny was forever changing his clothing in an attempt to have him look and smell presentable, a seemingly never-ending task. Yet we managed. We thrilled to every new milestone of his development, such as smiling and responding to our invitation for hand motions. We were proud parents and enjoyed his babyhood thoroughly.

While at home, Henny was anxious to assist by earning some extra money. She noticed that her friend, Jeanette Glass, typed addresses onto envelopes, at home, for which she was paid 2 cents per envelope. That seemed like easy money, so Henny obtained a box of 500 envelopes from Jeanette to do the same. 500 envelopes took every bit of the free time she had and when I came home from work she was completely exhausted. We agreed that she would stop after completing the batch, but she was proud of the $10 thus earned.

That summer we joined other members of our family for a week's vacation at a hotel at Asbury Park, New Jersey. Splashing in the hotel pool, supported by a rubber tube, David got his first real exposure to water in something bigger than a bathtub. We also had a thrill watching David enjoy his first kiddie rides and gingerly wading into the ocean surf. Henny, quite visibly pregnant with our second child, mostly observed as I seized this opportunity to bond with my son. I participated with him in every new activity, and for the first time, David rushed to me when he needed security or anything else. In the past he had normally run to his mommy. It's an exhilarating feeling when a new father first experiences an "on par with mother" relationship with his child. Today, perhaps quality time for fathers with their children is common, but in 1955, I experienced this as a quantum leap.

Shortly after 3 A.M. on October 21, Henny woke me to say that she had started to have labor pains. Although they were mild, they occurred at fairy regular intervals. The miracle of life happened to us for the second time. The baby was born early in the morning, at 4:15 A.M. after more than 24 hours of labor. "Congratulations, you have a healthy boy!"

Jonathan, however, weighed only 5 pounds 13 ounces. We decided to keep him in the hospital for eight days and have his circumcision there. Thereafter he came home to a joyous reception and an older brother gingerly admiring his new sibling.

Little Jonathan progressed nicely, and David played the roll of protective older brother. Time went on, and the boys grew according to the then-admired guidebook by Dr. Spock. Our savings slowly grew, too, and our lifestyle became a bit more affluent. We now enjoyed a TV set, a washing machine, a sewing machine, and in 1956, we bought our first car. The car gave us mobility so that we no longer were at the mercy of our friends and relatives when we wanted to go somewhere. Although I had a GI license, I had to take a civilian driving test. I took a brief refresher course and promptly flunked the driving test. My second try was successful. Now that we had a car, Henny was eager to learn how to drive. We decided that I would give her lessons. Since Henny was completely oblivious to the workings of an automobile, I explained to her how the gas and brake pedals worked and how, when you want to go to the right, you turned the steering wheel to the right and the front wheels would then turn to the right. Similarly, to go to the left you turned the steering wheel to the left, and the front wheels turned with it. Henny then asked, "How about the rear wheels, how do you turn them?" However, she diligently practiced with me, and when she took her road test she passed with flying colors at the first try.

In 1958, there were the first rumblings of change in our neighborhood. People in our apartment house were moving to the suburbs. Stories of local crime reports permeated the conversations. One evening while we were in our apartment, we heard someone scream. Looking out the window, we saw a distraught woman scream that someone had stolen her purse and run.

While concerns at home escalated, at Lester Associates we had secured a substantial contract to build exhibits for the New York State Power Authority. That fall, I spent more than a week at Massena, New York, supervising the installation of exhibits at the power dam named in Robert Moses's honor.

While I was away, I received a telephone call from Henny saying that David's school had burned down. As a consequence, he was being bussed to a school near 125th Street, in Harlem. It was not racial prejudice but quality of education that gave us concern. Unfortunately, good teachers do not want to teach in schools that have major discipline problems, drug problems, and overcrowding. David's new school suffered from all of these problems. In addition, the transportation, a lengthy trip via school bus, and the challenge of delivering him and picking him up at the bus stop, a considerable distance from our home, added to the stress. We started to talk about alternatives. The obvious one was to move.

A house in the suburbs with good schools and open spaces changed from a dream to a quest.

On weekends, working with local Realtors, we looked at new homes and resales. Based on our accumulated assets of about $8,000, my take home pay of $133 per week, and our current rent of $71 per month, we dared not spend more than $20,000 for a house. One of my co-workers, Joe Ivanick, who lived in Yonkers, told me of good housing available in Rockland County. This area had previously been considered too remote. Now, however, with the Tappan Zee Bridge recently completed and the Palisades Parkway under construction, this as yet underdeveloped area looked like it had a promising future. I came across an ad in the *New York Times* for "Spacious 7 ½ room ranch—Tudor Gate—West Nyack—priced $20,250—luxuriously proportioned rooms." We decided to take a look at that offering in West Nyack. As we arrived there, the sun was just starting to set. The lights in the model house were on and to me looked very inviting. Henny took one look at the exterior, however, and declared that she would rather not bother to get out of the car. The house looked like a summer bungalow to her. "Now that we are here why not take a look?"

"All right, but let's make it quick. It's getting dark and we don't really know this neighborhood. We don't want trouble finding our way home!"

We entered the model, and Henny's face lit up. It was charmingly furnished. The house looked bigger from the inside with a cathedral ceiling in the living room and the open floor plan connecting living room, dining room, and den. But most attractive was the kitchen layout with ample work space and a pleasant bay window eating area. The enclosed garage, rear patio, full basement, and three bedrooms with 1 ½ bathrooms and ample closet space all helped to convince us that this is what we had been looking for. It was not until early March of 1960 that we had our closing. On March 15, we bade farewell to our neighbors in New York and moved to West Nyack. A new phase of our life was about to begin.

The last snows of the season fell as the moving truck backed into our driveway at 15 Richard Drive. The new environment required some adjustment. There were no familiar faces. However, by April 22, David's 7th birthday, he had made enough friends in the immediate neighborhood to have them join him for a birthday party. Friendships developed rapidly with our fellow Tudor Gaters. Most of the residents were in our age group, had small children, and shared common interests. About half of the 50 new families were Jewish, but we mixed just as easily with most of the non-Jews. Our immediate neighbors, the Kriskes, were German and not Jewish. They had lived in Germany during World War II, and Otto Kriske had served in the German Army. Our contact with them was polite but limited until an event in early fall.

I, like most other new homeowners, mowed my own lawn. We had rain for several weeks prior to the Jewish holy day of Rosh Hashanah. I was thus unable to mow my grass. It had grown quite tall. On the first day of Rosh Hashanah, the weather was beautiful as we went to religious services. When we came home, our lawn was neatly cut. I wondered how this happened. Someone said he thought he saw my neighbor, Otto, do it. When I approached, Otto he told me that he knew I could not mow on my holy day, and since the weather was clear for a change, he cut the grass for me. I thanked him and realized that when people who have good intentions do a good deed, it is a sure sign of their goodness. We have been good friends ever since.

When we moved, we decided to have David and Jonathan share one bedroom so that we'd have an empty room in the event of another baby. Henny longed to have a baby girl, and we decided to try once more. In October of 1961, we had our new baby, a boy we named Daniel. Although Henny had hoped for a daughter, she was well satisfied with the nice healthy addition to our family, no matter what the sex. Life continued, quite mundane. Jonathan got a pet rabbit, which he promptly named Thumper. David had his tonsils removed. We purchased a set of World Book Encyclopedias and lived the American dream of a suburban life.

In 1967, Henny, in conversation with an acquaintance, learned that there were openings to teach half-day kindergarten in the local school district. Now that Daniel was in school, the idea of resuming her former career while also earning a little money appealed to her. She applied in person and was immediately offered a job. Somewhat taken aback, she responded that she'd like to review the matter with her husband. The next day she accepted the offer. It was an ideal job that would get her back home before the boys returned from school. The take-home pay was $208 per month. Not much of a salary, but she embraced her new work with enthusiasm and especially enjoyed the change of pace in her life.

In the fall of 1968, a new reality hit us: David was about to finish high school and was applying to college. Fortunately he was an excellent student. He aimed high and was accepted at the Massachusetts Institute of Technology.

In the summer of 1970, Henny and I took our first return trip to Europe, including a return visit to our ancestral villages,

Rehlingen and Battenberg. In Rehlingen, after a brief search, we located the house where Henny spent her early years. We parked our rented car and walked to the front door of the butcher store, wondering if it would be open since it was Sunday. It was open. As we entered, Henny felt an avalanche of emotions. Her memories were instantly refreshed by the unique green marble sales counter and the general appearance of the store, which had changed little since she lived there. The store was empty, but the bell that rang as we entered brought forth a young man who, speaking German, asked how he could help us. Henny quickly explained who she was and he, his emotions stirred, haltingly explained in German that he was the son of Alvis, the apprentice to Henny's father many years ago. The young man offered to fetch his father, who was nearby. In a few moments Alvis appeared with tears in his eyes. Was this really Henny, the little girl he used to carry around on his arm? Alvis was most cordial in showing us his family, the house, the garden, and the neighborhood. It seemed that he had completely forgotten the pain he caused back in 1935.

Henny's father had suggested, just before we went on this trip, that we visit one of his old friends. We asked Alvis for guidance and then walked to the friend's house. By coincidence, the old man was celebrating his 80th birthday that day, and his entire family had come to visit. What surprised us most was the behavior of several teenage boys who arrived to pay their respects. As was still their custom, they each made the rounds in the extremely crowded living room, shaking everyone's hand, bowing, and simultaneously clicking their heels. Before we left Rehlingen, the news of our arrival had spread, bringing several of Henny's ex-classmates to say hello and gawk at us. We left Rehlingen emotionally drained, pleased to have visited but with no desire ever to return.

Our travels included parts of France and southwest Germany, then on to Switzerland where we had a wonderful stay at Grindelwald. On to Bern, Lucerne, and Zurich, and then back to Germany. There we traveled along the "romantic road" to Rothenburg and then to Heidelberg, Frankfurt, and farther north to Battenberg.

I had no difficulty remembering the streets and locating the house of my childhood. Frau Hof, the widow of the man who had acquired our house and store, was cordial but nervous. She claimed to have little recollection of me but seemed to remember my mother, yet did not inquire about her. She acquiesced to show us the room in which I slept as a child and then offered us free range of the grounds around the house. She seemed mystified by our appearance and feared that we had intentions to somehow regain the property. After I explained that I was here strictly for sentimental reasons, she relaxed a little. We had initially planned to stay in Battenberg for another day and possibly look at other places and locate people I had known. But after viewing our house and then, in front of our house, the little park with the Hansel and Gretel fountain, still there, and the red Stürmer kiosk, now gone, we visited the cemetery where my father and grandfather are buried. What a shock! It was in a disgraceful condition. Vandalism was manifested by broken and overturned tombstones. Many tombstones seemed to be missing—gone. Everything was overgrown—nothing but brambles and weeds—a testament to complete lack of concern, not to mention respect. I said the traditional kadish prayer for the dead. Memories of my first kadish recitation almost 35 years before flashed through my mind. After we climbed over the deteriorated remnant of a fence, we studied our map for the quickest way out of Germany and on to Holland. All the ghosts of our German past revisited us as we left the country of our childhood memories.

Sightseeing in Holland, Belgium, and Luxembourg completed our tour. One of the last things we did was to visit the American Military Cemetery. Crosses row on row, intermingled with Stars of David, filled the field as far as the eye could see. How many young lives were snuffed out to rein in the fury of the Nazis?

When we returned to the United States and got back to work, business at Lester Associates was very slow. To keep the company going, the senior employees each took a working day per week off without pay. That inspired me to do some freelance work to supplement my income. Once started, I was able to do considerable work on my own. I stopped doing so only after Lester Associates became busy again. I saw the freelance effort as an excellent opportunity for Jonathan and David to work with me by helping on some of my projects. It also gave me an opportunity to teach them some of the skills I had acquired. There is a wonderful satisfaction in a cooperative effort between father and son.

In 1973, Jonathan was accepted by several colleges. We urged him to go to Cooper Union, a fine arts school, which is a 100 percent scholarship institution. However, he preferred Pratt Institute, which offered more courses in the field of his interest, motion picture film. Pratt awarded a very limited number of partial scholarships. Full (four-year) scholarships were awarded to only ten of the most promising applicants. To qualify, Jonathan had to submit an expanded portfolio, which he did. The quality as well as the diversity of his portfolio were undoubtedly the key, and we were proud and elated when he was awarded one of the ten full tuition scholarships.

In 1974, David applied to medical schools and was accepted at his first choice, Penn State's Hershey Medical School. He started there in 1975, the year my mother died. She had become increasingly ill, suffering from cancer of the intestines. The best efforts of the doctors at Columbia Medical Center were insufficient to halt her deteriorating condition. When all hope for her recovery was gone, we transferred her to Calvary Hospice where she expired on January 6. What a sad end to the life of such a noble person. We mourned, but the pain of a loss so great lingers for a long time if not forever. She was the bravest person I ever knew. She faced early widowhood, Nazi persecution, and the challenges of emigration with courage and determination. Throughout our struggles, she always offered positive support and munificent love. Sadly, the following August our family was hit with another loss. Henny's father died after a brief illness. He had reached the ripe age of 89 and had enjoyed the close proximity of his children throughout his life. We carried on without these two pillars of our family, and at the close of 1975, Henny and I celebrated our 25th wedding anniversary. Except for the recent losses, it had been a good 25 years, and we wished for another 25 which, in fact, was granted to us.

Henny and I took our first and very inspiring trip to Israel in 1978. This trip was a series of emotional highs that started the moment we landed to the strands of *Hatikvah* over the El Al aircraft P.A. system. We were emotionally touched by Massada, Jerusalem, and many other places we'd only read about in the Bible, as well as the "Good Fence" at the border with Lebanon where we stayed at a kibbutz just a few hundred feet from the Lebanese border.

Here, at the kibbutz, Christian Arabs and Jews worked together for each other's best interests. We thought that maybe here is the kernel of a solution for peace. Israel was a wonderful experience, but it did in no way detract from our affinity for the good old U.S.A. As before, we were thrilled when we landed safely back home at J.F.K. Airport. We celebrated our 50th anniversary on Monday December 25, 2000. As we went to bed that night, we cuddled up and reminisced about the 50 years we had spent together. We could never have imagined that we would be blessed by so many wonderful events in our life. We had traveled from dreadful persecution to the land of opportunity, and from near poverty to financial comfort. We own a modest but pleasant and comfortable home and enjoy our active retirement. We share our time with our many friends and our family, and most of all, we have an ever-deeper love for each other.

Fate, however, may not always be this kind to us in time to come. Eventually, we all must depart from life. I once read that our stories—our heritage—are the only things that remain when we die. We can leave property, money, jewelry, and other worldly goods, but none of those are truly lasting. The only thing that is constant is the thread of how we got to be who we are, and how our short time on Earth is connected to the people who came before and who will come after us.

This story ends here. I hope that I have given you a little understanding of our past. From it, perhaps you may gain some insight in how to conduct your own life so that it may ultimately bask in sunshine.

Progeny

David, Marilyn,
Rebecca and Mark

Jonathan, Kate,
Sonia and Owen

Daniel, Ann,
Amanda, Erica,
Melissa and
Joshua

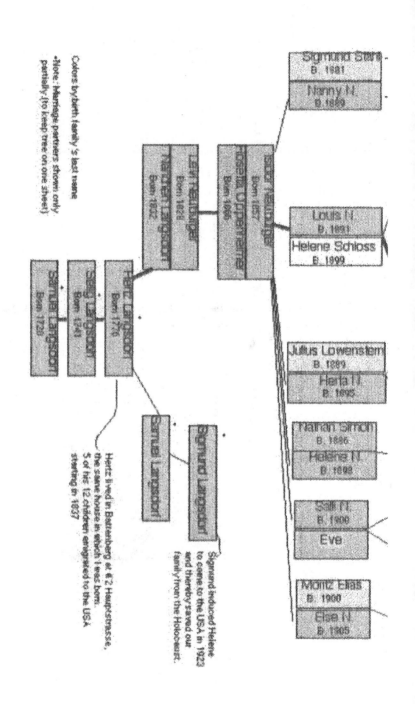

Colors by birth family's last name
*Note : Marriage partners shown only
partially (to keep tree on one sheet)

Sigmund Stern
B. 1881

Nanny N.
B. 1889

Kurt Neuhaus
Born 1826

Nathan Langsdorf
Born 1852

Julius Neuhaus
Born 1857

Rosalia Oppenheimer
Born 1855

Louis N.
B. 1891

Helene Schloss
B. 1899

Hertz Langsdorf
Born 1770

Seligman Langsdorf
Born 1741

Samuel Langsdorf
Born 1723

Julius Lowenstein
B. 1889

Herta N.
B. 1895

Nathan Simon
B. 1886

Helene N.
B. 1898

Salli N.
B. 1900

Eve

Moritz Elias
B. 1900

Else N.
B. 1905

Samuel Langsdorf

Sigmund Langsdorf

Hertz lived in Battenberg at #2 Hauptstrasse,
the same house in which I was born.
5 of his 12 children emigrated to the USA
starting in 1837

Sigmund induced Helene
to come to the USA in 1923
and thereby saved our
family from the Holocaust.